Auschwitz

A Doctor's Eyewitness Account

By DR. MIKLOS NYISZLI

TRANSLATED BY
TIBERE KREMER AND RICHARD SEAVER

WITH A FOREWORD BY
BRUNO BETTELHEIM

FAWCETT CREST • NEW YORK

TO MY WIFE AND DAUGHTER—

RETURNED FROM THE CAMP OF THE DEAD

AUSCHWITZ

THIS BOOK CONTAINS THE COMPLETE TEXT
OF THE ORIGINAL HARDCOVER EDITION.

Published by Fawcett Crest Books, a unit of CBS Publications,
the Consumer Publishing Division of CBS Inc.,
by arrangement with Frederick Fell, Inc.

ISBN: 0-449-23848-2

Printed in the United States of America.

24   23   22   21   20   19   18   17   16

"Many words have been written about the atrocities, terrors and sufferings that trademarked Nazi Germany's extermination camps . . . but none gives a more detailed picture than this account."

—*Hartford Times*

WHEN THE NAZIS INVADED Hungary in 1944, they shipped virtually the entire Jewish population to Auschwitz, the most infamous of all the concentration camps. There, separated from his family, Dr. Miklos Nyiszli was chosen to perform "scientific research" on his fellow prisoners—dead and alive. Miraculously, he survived—to write the most damning and shocking document yet to emerge from Eichmann's inferno.

FOREWORD

IT WAS WITH HESITATION THAT I ACCEPTED the invitation to write a foreword to this book. *Auschwitz,* beyond doubt, is an honest book, and an important one. It tells of events which, though gruesome, need to be told and retold until their meaning for our times is accepted. It is not a book for direct insight into the meaning of the extermination camps, but in the fate of the author lies much of its significance. Least of all, despite the author's claim, is it the book of a physician. Other physicians have written other books about their experiences in the concentration camps: for example, the psychiatrist Dr. Victor E. Frankl, who also wrote of Auschwitz. But Frankl did not help the SS in their experimentation on human beings; he did not pervert his calling by joining those who have aptly been called doctors of infamy. Instead of helping SS doctors in the killing of people, he suffered as a human being. Speaking of his experiences, he quotes Hebbel: "There are things which must cause one to lose one's reason, or one has none to lose." One of Dr. Nyiszli's fellow doctors did lose his reason, and the description of how it happened is not only one of the most moving parts of the book, but one of the most reassuring. There were, and still are, people who lose their reason when there is sufficient cause to do so.

Others did not lose their reason because, like Dr. Frankl, and thousands of other concentration camp prisoners, they never accepted their fate but fought it. Rightly, Dr. Nyiszli devotes much space to the men of the twelfth *Sonderkommando,* prisoners working in the gas chambers. Alone of all such commandos, it rediscovered freedom in the last days of its existence, and on the very last day regained it; therefore they died as men, not as living corpses. The account of this one *Sonderkommando* alone would make the book an important document. But its fate raises even more acutely the question of why only one of the fourteen such commandos fought back. Why did all others march themselves to their death? Why did millions of other prisoners do the same? Surely the story of these 800-odd men is a heroic saga of the extermination camps; it is a story that restores our trust in human beings. But they did only what we would expect all human beings to do: to use their death, if they could not save their lives, to weaken or hinder the enemy as much as possible; to use even their doomed selves for making extermination harder, or maybe impossible, not a smooth running process. Their story, then, remains within the human dimensions. If they could do it, so could others. Why didn't they? Why did they throw their lives away instead of making things hard for the enemy? Why did they make a present of their very being to the SS instead of to their families, their friends or even to fellow prisoners; this is the haunting question.

In its clues to an answer lies the importance of this book. It is an unbelievable story, but we all know it is true. We wish to forget it. It just does not fit into our system of value and thought. And rather than to reshape them, we wish to dismiss the story of the German extermination camps. If we could, we would prefer to think it never happened. The closest we can come to believing that is not to think about it so that we need not come to terms with its nightmarish perspectives.

The history of mankind, as of the Western world, abounds in persecutions for religious or political reasons. Large numbers of men were exterminated in other centuries too. Germany itself was depopulated by the Thirty Years War, during which millions of civilians died. And if two atomic bombs had not sufficed, maybe as many millions in Japan would have been exterminated as in the German extermination camps. War is horrible, and man's inhumanity to man even more so. Yet the importance of accounts on the extermination camps lies not in their all too familiar story but in something far more unusual and horrifying. It lies in a new dimension of man, an aspect we all wish to forget about, but forget only at our own risk. Strange as it may sound, the unique feature of the extermination camps is not that the Germans exterminated millions of people—that this is possible has been accepted in our picture of man, though not for centuries has it happened on that scale, and perhaps never with such callousness. What was new, unique, terrifying, was that millions, like lemmings, marched themselves to their own death. This is what is incredible; this we must come to understand.

Strangely enough, it was an Austrian who forged the tool for such understanding, and another Austrian whose acts forced an inescapable need to understand them upon us. Years before Hitler sent millions to the gas chambers, Freud insisted that human life is one long struggle against what he called the death instinct, and that we must learn to keep these destructive strivings within bounds lest they send us to our destruction. The twentieth century did away with ancient barriers that once prevented our destructive tendencies from running rampant, both in ourselves and in society. State, family, church, society, all were put to question, and found wanting. So their power to restrain or channel our destructive tendencies was weakened. The re-evaluation of all values which Nietzsche (Hitler's prophet, though Hitler, like others, misunderstood him abysmally) predicted would be required of Western man, were he to survive in the modern machine age, has not yet been achieved. The old means of controlling the death instinct have lost much of their hold, and the new, higher morality that should replace them is not yet achieved. In this interregnum between an old and new social organization—between man's obsolete inner organization and the new structure not yet achieved—little is left to restrain man's destructive tendencies. In this age then, only man's personal ability to control his own death instinct can protect him when the destructive forces of others, as in the Hitler state, run rampant.

This not being master of one's own death instinct can take many forms. The form it took in those extermination camp prisoners who walked themselves into the gas chambers began with their adherence to "business as usual." Those who tried to serve their executioners in what were once their civilian capacities (in this case, as physicians) were merely continuing if not business, then life as usual. Whereby they opened the door to their death.

Quite different was the reaction of those who did away with business as usual and would not join the SS in experimentation or extermination. Some of those who reported on the experience, desperately asked the question: How was it possible that people denied the existence of the gas chambers when all day long they saw the crematoria burning and smelled the odor of burning flesh? How come they preferred not to believe in the extermination just to prevent themselves from fighting for their very own lives? For example, Lengyel (in *Five Chimneys,* the story of Auschwitz, Chicago: Ziff Davis, 1947) reports that although she and her fellow prisoners lived just a few hundred yards from the crematoria and the gas chambers and knew what they were all about, yet after months most prisoners denied knowledge of them. German civilians denied the gas chambers too, but the same denial in them did not have the same meaning. Civilians who faced facts and rebelled, invited death. Prisoners at Auschwitz were already doomed. Rebellion could only have saved either the life they were going to lose anyway, or the lives of others. When Lengyel and many other prisoners were selected to be sent to the gas chambers, they did not try to break away, as she successfully did. Worse, the first time she tried it, some of the fellow prisoners selected with her for the gas chambers called the supervisors, telling them that Lengyel was trying to get away. Lengyel offers no explanation except that they begrudged anyone who might save himself from the common fate, because they lacked enough courage to risk action themselves. I believe they did it because they had given up their will to live, had permitted their death tendencies to flood them. As a result they now identified more closely with the SS who were devoting themselves to executing destructive tendencies, than to those fellow prisoners who still held a grip on life and hence managed to escape death.

But this was only a last step in giving up living one's own life, in no longer defying the death instinct which, in more scientific terms, has been called the principle of inertia. Because the first step was taken long before one entered the death camp. Inertia it was that led millions of Jews into the ghettos the SS created for them. It was inertia that made hundreds of thousands of Jews sit home, waiting for their executioners, when they were restricted to their homes. Those who did not allow inertia to take over used the imposing of such restrictions as a warning that it was high time to go underground, join resistance movements, provide themselves with forged papers, etc., if they had not done so long ago. Most of them survived. Again, inertia among non-Jews was not the same thing. It was not certain death that stared them in the face, but oppression. Submission, and a denial of the crimes of the Gestapo were, in their case, desperate efforts at survival. The remaining margin for a human existence shrank severely, but it existed. So one and the same pattern of behavior helped survival in one case, in the other did not; it was realistic behavior for Germans, self-delusion for Jews and for prisoners in the extermination camps, of whom a majority were Jews. When prisoners began to serve their executioners, to help them speed the death of their own kind, things had gone beyond simple inertia. By then, death instinct running rampant had been added to inertia.

Lengyel, too, mentions Dr. Mengele, one of the protagonists of *Auschwitz,* in a typical example of the "business as usual" attitude that enabled some prisoners, and certainly the SS, to retain whatever inner balance they could despite what they were doing. She describes how Dr. Mengele took all correct medical precautions during childbirth; for example, rigorously observing all aseptic principles, cutting the umbilical cord with greatest care, etc. But only half an hour later he sent mother and infant to be burnt in the crematorium.

The same business-as-usual attitude that enabled Dr. Nyiszli to function as a doctor in the camp, that motivated him to volunteer his help to the SS, enabled millions of Jews to live in ghettos where they not only worked for the Nazis but selected fellow Jews for them to send to the gas chambers. It was similar inertia if not also the "business-as-usual" attitude that postponed the uprising in the Warsaw ghetto till hardly any people or any strength was left for fighting, and certainly far too few to make a breakthrough that might have saved thousands of lives.

All this would be past history except that the very same business-as-usual is behind our trying to forget two things; that twentieth century men like us sent millions into the gas chambers, and that millions of men like us walked to their death without resistance. In Buchenwald, I talked to hundreds of German Jewish prisoners who were brought there in the fall of 1938. I asked them why they had not left Germany because of the utterly degrading and discriminating conditions they were subjected to. Their answer was: How could we leave? It would have meant giving up our homes, our places of business. Their earthly possessions had so taken possession of them that they could not move; instead of using them, they were run by them. As a matter of fact the discriminatory laws against the Jews were meant to force them to leave Germany, leaving most of their possessions behind. For a long time the intention of the Nazis was to force undesirable minorities, such as the Jews, into emigration. Only when this did not work was the extermination policy instituted, following also the inner logic of the Nazi racial ideology. But one wonders whether the notion that millions of Jews (and later foreign nationals) would submit to their extermination did not also result from seeing what degradation they were willing to accept without fighting back. The persecution of the Jews was aggravated, slow step by slow step, when no violent fighting back occurred. It may have been Jewish acceptance, without retaliatory fight, of ever harsher discrimination and degradation that first gave the SS the idea that they could be gotten to the point where they would walk to the gas chambers on their own. Most Jews in Poland who did not believe in business-as-usual survived the Second World War. As the Germans approached, they left everything behind and fled to Russia, much as many of them distrusted the Soviet system. But there, while perhaps citizens of a second order, they were at least accepted as human beings. Those who stayed on to continue business-as-usual moved toward their own destruction and perished. Thus in the deepest sense the walk to the gas chamber was only the last consequence of a philosophy of business-as-usual: True, the same suicidal behavior has another meaning. It means that man can be pushed so far and no further; that beyond a certain point he chooses death to an inhuman existence. But the initial step toward this terrible choice was the inertia that preceded it.

Perhaps a remark on the universal success of the *Diary of Anne Frank* may stress how much we all wish to subscribe to this business-as-usual philosophy, and to forget that it hastens our destruction. It is an onerous task to take apart such a humane, such a moving story that arouses so much compassion for gentle Anne Frank. But I believe that the worldwide acclaim of her story cannot be explained unless we recognize our wish to forget the gas chambers and to glorify the attitude of going on with business-as-usual, even in a holocaust. While the Franks were making their preparations for going passively into hiding, thousands of other Jews in Holland and elsewhere in Europe were trying to escape to the free world, the better to be able to fight their executioners. Others who could not do so went underground—not simply to hide from the SS, waiting passively, without preparation for fight, for the day when they would be caught—but to fight against the Germans, and for humanity. All the Franks wanted was to go on with life as much as possible in the usual fashion. Little Anne, too, wanted only to go on with life as usual, and nobody can blame her. But hers was certainly not a necessary fate, much less a heroic one; it was a senseless fate. The Franks could have faced the facts and survived, as did many Jews living in Holland. Anne could have had a good chance to survive, as did many Jewish children in Holland. But for that she would have had to be separated from her parents and gone to live with a Dutch family as their own child. Everybody who recognized the obvious knew that the hardest way to go underground was to do it as a family; that to hide as a family made detection by the SS most likely. The Franks, with their excellent connections among gentile Dutch families should have had an easy time hiding out singly, each with a different family. But instead of planning for this, the main principle of their planning was to continue as much as possible with the kind of family life they were accustomed to. Any other course would have meant not merely giving up the beloved family life as usual, but also accepting as reality man's inhumanity to man. Most of all it would have forced their acceptance that business-as-usual was not an absolute value, but can sometimes be the most destructive of all attitudes. There is little doubt that the Franks, who were able to provide themselves with so much, could have provided themselves with a gun or two had they wished. They could have shot down at least one or two of the SS men who came for them. There was no surplus of SS men. The loss of an SS with every Jew arrested would have noticeably hindered the functioning of the police state. The fate of the Franks wouldn't have been any different, because they all died anyway except for Anne's father, though he hardly meant to pay for his survival with the extermination of his whole family. They could have sold their lives dearly instead of walking to their death.

There is good reason why the so successful play ends with Anne stating her belief in the good in all men. What is denied is the importance of accepting the gas chambers as real so that never again will they exist. If all men are basically good, if going on with intimate family living no matter what else is what is to be most admired, then indeed we can all go on with life as usual and forget about Auschwitz. Except that Anne Frank died because her parents could not get themselves to believe in Auschwitz. And her story found wide acclaim because for us too, it denies implicitly that Auschwitz ever existed. If all men are good, there can be no Auschwitz.

I have met many Jews, as well as gentile anti-Nazis, who survived in Germany and in the occupied countries. But they were all people who realized that when a world goes to pieces, when inhumanity reigns supreme, man cannot go on with business as usual. One then has to radically re-evaluate all of what one has done, believed in, stood for. In short, one has to take a stand on the new reality, a firm stand, and not one of retirement into even greater privatization.

If today, Negroes in Africa march against the guns of a police that defends *apartheid*—even if hundreds of them will be shot down and tens of thousands rounded up in concentration camps—their march, their fight, will sooner or later assure them of a chance for liberty and equality. The Jews of Europe could equally have marched as free men against the SS, rather than to first grovel, then wait to be rounded up for their own extermination, and finally walk themselves to the gas chambers. It was their passive waiting for the SS to knock at their door without first securing a gun to shoot down at least one SS before being shot down themselves, that was the first step in a voluntary walk into the Reich's crematoria.

While all other accounts of the concentration camps that have come to my attention were by persons who never willingly served the SS, to my knowledge Dr. Nyiszli's is the only report written by one of the many concentration camp prisoners who volunteered to become a tool of the SS to stay alive. But having made his choice, Dr. Nyiszli had, after all, to delude himself at times to be able to live with himself and his experience. And herein lies the true importance of this document for the protection that understanding can offer. Because even in the overpowering setting of Auschwitz, certain defenses still served life, not the death instinct. Most important of these was understanding what went on in oneself, and why. With enough understanding, the individual did not fool himself into believing that saving his skin was the same as saving the total self. He was able to recognize that much of what apparently seemed protective was actually self destroying.

A most extreme example were those prisoners who volunteered to work in the gas chambers hoping it would somehow save their lives. All of them were killed after a short time. But many of them died sooner, and after weeks of a more horrible life, than might have been true if they had not volunteered.

How Dr. Nyiszli fooled himself can be seen, for example, in his repeatedly referring to his work as a doctor, though he worked as the assistant of a vicious criminal. He speaks of the Institute for Race, Biological, and Anthropological Investigation as "one of the most qualified medical centers of the Third Reich" though it was devoted to proving falsehoods. That the author was a doctor didn't at all change the fact that he, like any of the prisoner officials who served the SS better than some SS were willing to serve it, was a participant, an accessory to the crimes of the SS. How then could he do it and survive? By taking pride in his professional skills, irrespective of what purpose they were used for. Again and again this pride in his professional skill permeates his story of his and other prisoners' sufferings. The important issue here is that Dr. Nyiszli, Dr. Mengele and hundreds of other far more prominent physicians, men trained long before the advent of Hitler to power, were participants in these human experiments and in the pseudo-scientific investigations that went with them. It is this pride in professional skill and knowledge, irrespective of moral implications, that is so dangerous. As a feature of modern society oriented toward technological competence it is still with us, though the concentration camps, the crematoria, the extermination of millions because of race, are no longer here. Auschwitz is gone, but as long as this attitude remains with us we shall not be safe from the criminal indifference to life at its core.

I recommend to careful reading the description of how the first task of every new *Sonderkommando* was to cremate the corpses of the preceding *kommando,* exterminated just a few hours before. I recommend to the reader's speculation why, though the twelfth *Sonderkommando* revolted, the thirteenth went quietly to its death without opposition.

In this single revolt of the twelfth *Sonderkommando,* seventy SS were killed, including one commissioned officer and seventeen non-commissioned officers; one of the crematoria was totally destroyed and another severely damaged. True, all eight hundred and fifty-three prisoners of the *kommando* died. But this proves that a position in the *Sonderkommando* gave prisoners a chance of about ten to one to destroy the SS, a higher ratio than existed in the ordinary concentration camp. The one *Sonderkommando* that revolted and took such heavy toll of the enemy did not die much differently than all other *Sonderkommandos.* Why, then—and this is the question that haunts all who study the extermination camps—why then did millions walk quietly, without resistance to their death when right before them were examples such as this commando that managed to destroy and damage its own death chambers and kill 10% of their own number in SS? Why did so few of the millions of prisoners die like men, as did the men of only one of these commandos?

Perhaps comparing the two physicians who survived Auschwitz may suggest an answer. Dr. Frankl, who during imprisonment searched continuously for the personal meaning of his experience as a concentration camp prisoner, thereby found the deeper meaning of his life and life in general. Other prisoners who, like Doctor Nyiszli, were concerned with mere survival—even if it meant helping SS doctors in their nefarious experiments with human beings—gained no deeper meaning from their horrible experience. And so they survived in body, haunted by remorse and nightmarish recollections.

This book then is most of all a cautionary tale, as old as mankind. Those who seek to protect the body at all cost die many times over. Those who risk the body to survive as men have a good chance to live on.

—BRUNO BETTELHEIM

University of Chicago
May, 1960

INTRODUCTION

In MID-MARCH OF 1944 THE GERMANS IN-
vaded Hungary. All Jews were immediately
consigned to house-arrest; deportations be-
gan soon afterwards. In April, together with all the Jews
of his city, Dr. Miklos Nyiszli was shipped to Auschwitz.

Separated from his wife and daughter upon arrival,
Dr. Nyiszli was chosen by the evil master mind of the
Auschwitz crematoriums, Obersturmführer Dr. Mengele,
to take charge of all the pathological work carried on in
the camp. As such, Dr. Nyiszli became a member of the
Sonderkommando, the specially qualified and privileged
group of prisoners who worked exclusively inside the crematoriums. This Sonderkommando, also known as the
"kommando of the living dead," consisted of some 860
male prisoners chosen for their professional abilities, their
strength and good constitution. As long as they lived their
lot was relatively good, but they lived for only four months
from the time they entered the crematorium: at the end of
that brief period they were liquidated and replaced by a
new group of prisoners.

In this way the Nazis hoped to keep from the world
any knowledge of the heinous deeds perpetrated in these
"death factories." They very nearly succeeded: of the
several stories and documents based on life in the KZ—
the concentration camps—none, to my knowledge, has
ever recounted in detail the conditions inside the crematoriums, for the simple reason that the gate to the crematoriums was the gate to death.

Almost miraculously, Dr. Nyiszli survived. Through his
eyes we relive not only the day-to-day horrors of life in
the KZ, but also witness the slow disintegration of an
empire built to last a thousand years. For the picture that
unfolds beneath the doctor's untutored pen spans the
period from the orderly "selections," the methodical ex-
terminations of early 1944, to the nightmarish exodus that
marked Germany's collapse in the spring of 1945. I say
"untutored pen" because, as Dr. Nyiszli himself states:
"When I lived through these horrors, which are beyond all
imagining, I was not a writer but a doctor. Today, in

writing about them, I write not as a reporter but as a doctor." Those looking for a well-constructed story, for elegance of style or literary expression will be disappointed here, perhaps even irritated at times by the doctor's sometimes hyperbolic, impressionistic account of his experience. But in a book of this nature the raw material is all that matters.

What Dr. Nyiszli lived through and witnessed few will believe, or want to believe, for the human mind inevitably turns away from suffering and whatever is repugnant. From that to denying that such treatment and torture as are here described could really have existed is but a simple step to take. But the fact remains they did exist.

But why, one may well ask, force such a document of suffering on the public, why rake cold ashes, stir up old animosities? Would it not be better to forget the past? Fair questions, to be sure, and perhaps it would indeed be preferable not to reawaken such memories. Those who lived through the concentration camps do not talk readily about their experiences. I have met several who were interned at Dachau and Bergen-Belsen and Auschwitz, and rarely if ever have they talked openly of those frightful years. Most have returned to their homes and worked to rebuild their lives as best they could. Some have died, months or years after their liberation, from illnesses resulting directly from their confinement. Illnesses as often mental as physical: one girl I met, only sixteen at the time she was freed, committed suicide in Paris in 1954, almost ten years after her liberation. She had returned to civilization, married, had a young son she adored, was quite well off financially and, a strong-willed person, apparently completely restored. But six months before her death she had a breakdown, was kept under constant surveillance, but steadily declined until, after several abortive attempts, she succeeded in escaping her past. As much as those who died before the SS machine guns or in the gas chambers, she was a belated victim of the KZ.

But it is neither to condemn a race for past crimes nor to solicit sympathy for those who suffered, or still suffer today, that we have undertaken to bring this document before the English-speaking public. Rather, it is because, as Meyer Levin once pointed out, "These victims of Nazi atrocities hid fragmentary records of their experience, they scratched words on walls, they died hoping the world would some day know, not in statistics but in empathy. We are charged to listen." [1] Moreover, a book such as this may serve to remind us, in spite of the distance separating us from the nightmare it describes, of what the by-products of war can be, of what, when societies allow themselves to be lulled and led by facile formulas based on hate and disdain, man is capable of inflicting on his fellow being.

Even in a world of "cold war," and of hot "fringe wars," to most of us such callous treatment of man by his fellow being seems inconceivable. And yet out of Korea and Indochina and North Africa have come stories just as sordid as the one you are about to read. The welter of claims and counter claims makes it difficult to lay the blame, or limit it exclusively to one side. But it is not the censuring of the perpetrators of atrocities that matters, really, but the continued existence of the atrocities themselves. "Let no man think himself, or his race, superior": *Auschwitz* constantly reminds us, however indirectly at times, of this cogent thought. For without the theory of the Master Race the horrors of the concentration camps could never have existed. The theory of Aryan supremacy was more than a pretext to liquidate the Jews of Europe: many, too many, seduced by this ugly propaganda, grew to believe it ardently. Thus sending bullets into the backs of a hundred necks, or standing by as thousands of men, women and children were herded into the gas chambers, needed no justification. As members of the Master Race the officials of Nazi Germany were merely fulfilling their sacred duty.

The danger is collective; the responsibility is individual. Even those who did not contribute directly to the atrocities but who knew, however vaguely, that they existed, are guilty. The swastika, like the burning cross, thrives in an ambiance of fear and hate. But it counts apathy as an indispensable ally.

Now the swastika has appeared again on temple walls throughout the world, reminding us that it has not been eradicated, as we had blandly assumed. If we are apathetic enough, if we dismiss it as the work of irresponsible hoodlums (Hitler and his henchmen were long dismissed

[1] *New York Times Book Review*, May 8, 1955.

as irresponsible hoodlums) it can, like the cancer it is, grow and spread. If the present document contributes in some small measure to the dissipation of that dangerous apathy, it will have served its purpose.

We have also unlocked the secret of universal suicide. It is not impossible that this realization has kept the world in relative peace since Auschwitz was destroyed fifteen years ago. It is not impossible that this realization will keep the world at peace in the decades to come, so that man can direct his energies towards good rather than evil, towards dignifying life rather than destroying it. Only if this happens will the unnumbered millions, who suffered and perished in the course of these wars, not have died wholly in vain.

—RICHARD SEAVER

New York
April, 1960

DECLARATION

I, THE UNDERSIGNED, DR. MIKLOS NYISZLI, physician, former prisoner of the German concentration camps, declare that this work, which relates the darkest days in the history of mankind, was drawn up by me in strict accordance with reality, and without the slightest exaggeration, in my capacity as an eyewitness and involuntary participant in the work of the Auschwitz crematoriums, into whose fires millions of fathers, mothers and children disappeared.

As chief physician of the Auschwitz crematoriums, I drafted numerous affidavits of dissection and forensic medicine findings which I signed with my own tattoo number. I sent these documents by mail, counter signed by my superior, Dr. Mengele, to the Berlin-Dahlem address of the "Institut für Rassenbiologische und Anthropologische Forschungen," one of the most qualified medical centers of the Third Reich. It should still be possible to find them today in the archives of this Research Institute.

In writing this work I am not aiming for any literary success. When I lived through these horrors, which were beyond all imagining, I was not a writer but a doctor. Today, in telling about them, I write not as a reporter but as a doctor.

Done at Oradea-Nagyvarad, March 1946.

Signed:
Dr. Miklos Nyiszli

1 May, 1944. INSIDE EACH OF THE LOCKED cattle cars ninety people were jammed. The stench of the urinal buckets, which were so full they overflowed, made the air unbreathable.

The train of the deportees. For four days, forty identical cars had been rolling endlessly on, first across Slovakia, then across the territory of the Central Government, bearing us towards an unknown destination. We were part of the first group of over a million Hungarian Jews condemned to death.

Leaving Tatra behind us, we passed the stations of Lublin and Krakau. During the war these two cities were used as regroupment camps—or, more exactly, as extermination camps—for here all the anti-Nazis of Europe were herded and sorted out for extermination.

Scarcely an hour out of Krakau the train ground to a halt before a station of some importance. Signs in Gothic letters announced it as "Auschwitz," a place which meant nothing to us, for we had never heard of it.

Peering through a crack in the side of the car, I noticed an unusual bustle taking place about the train. The SS troops who had accompanied us till now were replaced by others. The trainmen left the train. From chance snatches of conversation overheard I gathered we were nearing the end of our journey.

The line of cars began to move again, and some twenty minutes later stopped with a prolonged, strident whistle of the locomotive.

Through the crack I saw a desert-like terrain: the earth was a yellowish clay, similar to that of Eastern Silesia, broken here and there by a green thicket of trees. Concrete pylons stretched in even rows to the horizon, with barbed wire strung between them from top to bottom. Signs warned us that the wires were electrically charged with high tension current. Inside the enormous squares bounded by the pylons stood hundreds of barracks, cov-

21

ered with green tar-paper and arranged to form a long,
rectangular network of streets as far as the eye could see.

Tattered figures, dressed in the striped burlap of prisoners, moved about inside the camp. Some were carrying
planks, others were wielding picks and shovels, and, farther on, still others were hoisting fat trunks onto the
backs of waiting trucks.

The barbed wire enclosure was interrupted every thirty
or forty yards by elevated watch towers, in each of which
an SS guard stood leaning against a machine gun mounted
on a tripod. This then was the Auschwitz concentration
camp, or, according to the Germans, who delight in ab-
breviating everything, the KZ, pronounced "Katzet." Not
a very encouraging sight to say the least, but for the
moment our awakened curiosity got the better of our fear.

I glanced around the car at my companions. Our group
consisted of some twenty-six doctors, six pharmacists, six
women, our children, and some elderly people, both men
and women, our parents and relatives. Seated on their
baggage or on the floor of the car, they looked both tired
and apathetic, their faces betraying a sort of foreboding
that even the excitement of our arrival was unable to
dispel. Several of the children were asleep. Others sat
munching the few scraps of food we had left. And the
rest, finding nothing to eat, were vainly trying to wet their
desiccated lips with dry tongues.

Heavy footsteps crunched on the sand. The shout of
orders broke the monotony of the wait. The seals on the
cars were broken. The door slid slowly open and we
could already hear them giving us orders.

"Everyone get out and bring his hand baggage with
him. Leave all heavy baggage in the cars."

We jumped to the ground, then turned to take our
wives and children in our arms and help them down, for
the level of the cars was over four and a half feet from
the ground. The guards had us line up along the tracks.
Before us stood a young SS officer, impeccable in his
uniform, a gold rosette gracing his lapel, his boots smartly
polished. Though unfamiliar with the various SS ranks,
I surmised from his arm band that he was a doctor. Later
I learned that he was the head of the SS group, that his
name was Dr. Mengele, and that he was chief physician
of the Auschwitz concentration camp. As the "medical

selector" for the camp, he was present at the arrival of every train.

In the moments that followed we experienced certain phases of what, at Auschwitz, was called "selection." As for the subsequent phases, everyone lived through them according to his particular fate.

To start, the SS quickly divided us according to sex, leaving all children under fourteen with their mothers. So our once united group was straightway split in two. A feeling of dread overwhelmed us. But the guards replied to our anxious questions in a paternal, almost good-natured manner. It was nothing to be concerned about. They were being taken off for a bath and to be disinfected, as was the custom. Afterwards we would all be reunited with our families.

While they sorted us out for transportation I had a chance to look around. In the light of the dying sun the image glimpsed earlier through the crack in the box car seemed to have changed, grown more eery and menacing. One object immediately caught my eye: an immense square chimney, built of red bricks, tapering towards the summit. It towered above a two-story building and looked like a strange factory chimney. I was especially struck by the enormous tongues of flame rising between the lightning rods, which were set at angles on the square tops of the chimney. I tried to imagine what hellish cooking would require such a tremendous fire. Suddenly I realized that we were in Germany, the land of the crematory ovens. I had spent ten years in this country, first as a student, later as a doctor, and knew that even the smallest city had its crematorium.

So the "factory" was a crematorium. A little farther on I saw a second building with its chimney; then, almost hidden in a thicket, a third, whose chimneys were spewing the same flames. A faint wind brought the smoke towards me. My nose, then my throat, were filled with the nauseating odor of burning flesh and scorched hair. —Plenty of food for thought there. But meanwhile the second phase of selection had begun. In single file, men, women, children, the aged, had to pass before the selection committee.

Dr. Mengele, the medical "selector," made a sign. They lined up again in two groups. The left-hand column included the aged, the crippled, the feeble, and women with children under fourteen. The right-hand column consisted entirely of able-bodied men and women: those able to work. In this latter group I noticed my wife and fourteen-year-old daughter. We no longer had any way of speaking to each other; all we could do was make signs.

Those too sick to walk, the aged and insane, were loaded into Red Cross vans. Some of the elderly doctors in my group asked if they could also get into the vans. The trucks departed, then the left-hand group, five abreast, flanked by SS guards, moved off in its turn. In a few minutes they were out of sight, cut off from view by a thicket of trees.

The right-hand column had not moved. Dr. Mengele ordered all doctors to step forward; he then approached the new group, composed of some fifty doctors, and asked those who had studied in a German university, who had a thorough knowledge of pathology and had practiced forensic medicine, to step forward.

"Be very careful," he added. "You must be equal to the task; for if you're not . . ." and his menacing gesture left little to the imagination. I glanced at my companions. Perhaps they were intimidated. What did it matter! My mind was already made up.

I broke ranks and presented myself. Dr. Mengele questioned me at length, asking me where I had studied, the names of my pathology professors, how I had acquired a knowledge of forensic medicine, how long I had practiced, etc. Apparently my answers were satisfactory, for he immediately separated me from the others and ordered my colleagues to return to their places. For the moment they were spared. Because I must now state a truth of which I then was ignorant, namely, that the left-hand group, and those who went off in cars, passed a few moments later through the doors of the crematorium. From which no one ever returned.

2 STANDING ALONE, A LITTLE APART FROM the others, I fell to thinking about the strange and devious ways of fate, and, more precisely, about Germany, where I had spent some of the happiest years of my life.

Now, above my head, the sky was bright with stars, and the soft evening breeze would have been refreshing if, from time to time, it had not borne with it the odor of bodies burning in the Third Reich's crematoriums.

Hundreds of searchlights strung on top of the concrete pillars shone with a dazzling brilliance. And yet, behind the chain of lights, it seemed as though the air had grown heavier, enveloping the camp in a thick veil, through which only the blurred silhouettes of the barracks showed.

By now the cars were empty. Some men, dressed in prison garb, arrived and unloaded the heavy baggage we had left behind, then loaded it onto waiting trucks. In the gathering darkness the forty box cars slowly faded, till at last they melted completely into the surrounding countryside.

Dr. Mengele, having issued his final instructions to the SS troops, crossed to his car, climbed in behind the wheel and motioned for me to join him. I got into the back seat beside an SS junior officer and we started off. The car bounced crazily along the clay roads of the camp, which were rutted and filled with potholes from the spring rains. The bright searchlights flew past us, faster and faster, and in a short while we stopped before an armored gate. From his post an SS sentry came running up to let the familiar car through. We drove a few hundred yards farther along the main road of the camp, which was bounded on either side by barracks, then stopped again in front of a building which was in better shape than the others. A sign beside the entrance informed me that this was the "Camp Office."

Inside several people, with deep, intelligent eyes and refined faces, wearing the uniform of prisoners, sat working at their desks. They immediately rose and came to attention. Dr. Mengele crossed to one of them, a man of about fifty, whose head was shaved clean. Since I was standing a few steps behind the Obersturmführer, it was impossible for me to hear what they were saying. Dr. Sentkeller, a prisoner, and, as I later learned, the F Camp doctor, nodded his head in assent. At his request, I approached another prisoner's desk. The clerk rummaged for some file cards, then asked me a number of questions about myself, recorded the answers both on the card and in a large book, and handed the card to an SS guard. Then we left the room. As I passed in front of Dr. Mengele I bowed slightly. Observing this, Dr. Sentkeller could not refrain from raising his voice and remarking, ironically rather than with intended malice, that such civilities were not the custom here, and that one would do well not to play the man of the world in the KZ.

A guard took me to another barracks, on the entrance to which was written: "Baths & Disinfection," where I and my card were turned over to still another guard. A prisoner approached me and took my medical bag, then searched me and told me to undress. A barber came over and shaved first my head, then the rest of my body, and sent me to the showers. They rubbed my head with a solution of calcium chloride, which burnt my eyes so badly that for several minutes I could not open them again.

In another room my clothes were exchanged for a heavy, almost new jacket, and a pair of striped trousers. They gave me back my shoes after having dipped them in a tank containing the same solution of calcium chloride. I tried on my new clothes and found they fitted me quite well. (I wondered what poor wretch had worn them before me.) Before I could reflect any further, however, another prisoner pulled up my left sleeve and, checking the number on my card, began skillfully to make a series of little tattoo marks on my arm, using an instrument filled with a blue ink. A number of small, bluish spots appeared almost immediately. "Your arm will swell a little," he reassured me, "but in a week that will disappear and the number will stand out quite clearly."

So I, Dr. Miklos Nyiszli, had ceased to exist; henceforth I would be, merely, KZ prisoner Number A 8450.

Suddenly I recalled another scene; fifteen years before, the Rector of the Medical School of Frederick Wilhelm University in Breslau shook my hand and wished me a brilliant future as he handed me my diploma, "with the congratulations of the jury."

3 FOR THE MOMENT MY SITUATION WAS TOLerable. Dr. Mengele expected me to perform the work of a physician. I would probably be sent to some German city as a replacement for a German doctor who had been drafted into military service, and whose functions had included pathology and forensic medicine. Moreover, I was filled with hope by the fact that, by Dr. Mengele's orders, I had not been issued a prisoner's burlap, but an excellent suit of civilian clothes.

It was already past midnight, but my curiosity kept me from feeling tired. I listened carefully to the barracks chief's every word. He knew the complete organization of the KZ, the names of the SS commanders in each camp section, as well as those of the prisoners who occupied important posts. I learned that the Auschwitz KZ was not a work camp, but the largest extermination camp in the Third Reich. He also told me of the "selections" that were made daily in the hospitals and the barracks. Hundreds of prisoners were loaded every day onto trucks and transported to the crematoriums, only a few hundred yards away.

From his tales I learned of life in the barracks. Eight hundred to a thousand people were crammed into the superimposed compartments of each barracks. Unable to stretch out completely, they slept there both lengthwise and crosswise, with one man's feet on another's head, neck, or chest. Stripped of all human dignity, they pushed and shoved and bit and kicked each other in an effort to get a few more inches' space on which to sleep a little more comfortably. For they did not have long to sleep:

reveille sounded at three in the morning. Then guards, armed with rubber clubs, drove the prisoners from their "beds." Still half asleep, they poured from the barracks, elbowing and shoving, and immediately lined up outside. Then began the most inhumane part of the KZ program: roll call. The prisoners were standing in rows of five. Those in charge arranged them in order. The barracks clerk lined them up by height, the taller ones in front and the shorter behind. Then another guard arrived, the day's duty guard for the section, and he, lashing out with his fists as he went, pushed the taller men back and had the short men brought up front. Then, finally, the barracks leader arrived, well dressed and well fed. He too was dressed in prison garb, but his uniform was clean and neatly pressed. He paused and haughtily scanned the ranks to see if everything was in order. Naturally it was not, so he began swinging with closed fists at those in the front rank who were wearing glasses, and drove them into the back rank. Why? Nobody knew. In fact you did not even think about it, for this was the KZ, and no one would even think of hunting for a reasonable explanation for such acts.

This sport continued for several hours. They counted the rows of men more than fifteen times, from front to back and back to front and in every other possible direction they could devise. If a row was not straight the entire barracks remained squatting for an hour, their hands raised above their heads, their legs trembling with fatigue and cold. For even in summer the Auschwitz dawns were cold, and the prisoners' light burlap served as scant protection against the rain and cold. But, winter and summer, roll call began at 3:00 A.M. and ended at 7:00, when the SS officers arrived.

The barracks leader, an obsequious servant of the SS, was invariably a common law criminal, whose green insignia distinguished him from the other prisoners. He snapped to attention and made his report, giving a muster of those men under his command. Next it was the turn of the SS to inspect the ranks: they counted the columns and inscribed the numbers in their notebooks. If there were any dead in the barracks—and there were generally five or six a day, sometimes as many as ten—they too had to be present for the inspection. And not only present in name, but physically present, standing, stark naked, supported by two living prisoners until the muster was over. For, living or dead, the prescribed number of prisoners had to be present and accounted for. It sometimes happened that when they were overworked, the kommando whose job it was to transport the dead in wheelbarrows failed to pass by for several days. Then the dead had to be brought to each inspection until the transportation kommando finally arrived to take charge of them. Only then were their names crossed off the muster list.

After all I had learned, I was not sorry to have acted boldly and tried to better my lot. By having been chosen, the very first day, to work as a doctor, I had been able to escape the fate of being lost in the mass and drowned in the filth of the quarantine camp.[1]

Thanks to my civilian clothes, I had managed to maintain a human appearance, and this evening I would sleep in the medical room bed of the twelfth "hospital" barracks.

At seven in the morning: reveille. The doctors in my section, as well as the personnel of the hospital, lined up in front of the barracks to be counted. That took about two or three minutes. They also counted the bed-ridden, as well as the previous night's dead. Here too the dead were stretched out beside the living.

During breakfast, which we took in our rooms, I met my colleagues. The head doctor of barracks-hospital number 12 was Dr. Levy, professor at the University of Strasbourg; his associate was Dr. Gras, professor at the University of Zagreb; both were excellent practitioners, known throughout Europe for their skill.

With practically no medicines, working with defective instruments and in surroundings where the most elementary aseptics and antiseptics were lacking, unmindful of their personal tragedy, unconscious of fatigue and danger, they did their best to care for the sick, and ease the sufferings of their fellow men.

In the Auschwitz KZ the healthiest individual was given three or four weeks to collapse from hunger, filth, blows and inhuman labor. How can one describe the

---

[1] The quarantine camp was that area to which the prisoners selected for the right-hand column were first sent. They were kept there till they had bathed, been disinfected and shaved, and had traded their civilian clothes for a prisoner's burlap. Later they were sent to various sections throughout the camp.—Tr.

state of those who were already organically ill when they reached the camp? In circumstances where it was difficult to forget that one was a human being, and a doctor besides, they practiced their profession with complete devotion. Their example was faithfully followed by the subaltern medical corps, which was composed of six doctors. They were all young French or Greek doctors. For three years they had been eating the KZ bread made from wild chestnuts sprinkled with sawdust. Their wives, their children, their relatives and friends had been liquidated upon arrival. Or rather, burned. If by chance they had been directed to the right-hand column they had been unable to stand up under the ordeal for more than two or three months and, as the "chosen," had disappeared into the flames.

Overcome by despair, resigned, apathetic, they nevertheless attempted, with the utmost devotion, to help the living-dead whose fate was in their hands. For the prisoners of that hospital *were* the living-dead. One had to be seriously ill before being admitted to the KZ hospital. For the most part they were living skeletons: dehydrated, emaciated, their lips were cracked, their faces swollen, and they had incurable dysentery. Their bodies were covered with enormous and repulsive running sores and suppurating ulcers. Such were the KZ's sick. Such were those one had to care for and comfort.

4   I STILL HAD NO CLEARLY DEFINED JOB. During a visit around the camp in the company of a French doctor, I noticed a sort of annex jutting out from one side of a KZ barracks. From the outside it looked like a toolshed. Inside, however, I saw a table about as high as a man's head, built of unplaned, rather thick boards; a chair; a box of dissecting instruments; and, in one corner, a pail. I asked my colleague what it was used for.

"That's the KZ's only dissecting room," he said. "It

hasn't been used for some time. As a matter of fact, I don't know of any specialist in the camp who's qualified to perform dissections, and I wouldn't be a bit surprised to learn that your presence here is tied in with Dr. Mengele's plans for reactivating it."

The very thought dampened my spirits, for I had pictured myself working in a modern dissecting room, not in this camp shed. In the course of my entire medical career I had never had to work with such defective instruments as these, or in a room so primitively equipped. Even when I had been called into the provinces on cases of murder and suicide, where the autopsy had had to be performed on the spot, I had been better equipped and installed.

Nevertheless I resigned myself to the inevitable, and accepted even this eventuality, for in the KZ this was still a favored position. And yet I still could not understand why I had been given almost new civilian clothes if I were slated to work in a dirty shed. It didn't make sense. But I decided not to waste my time worrying about such apparent contradictions.

Still in the company of my French colleague, I gazed out across the barbed wire enclosures. Naked dark-skinned children were running and playing. Women with Creole-like faces and gaily colored clothes, and half-naked men, seated on the ground in groups, chatted as they watched the children play. This was the famous "Gypsy Camp." The Third Reich's ethnological experts had classified gypsies as an inferior race. Accordingly, they had been rounded up, not only in Germany itself, but throughout the occupied countries, and herded here. Because they were Catholics, they were allowed the privilege of remaining in family groups.

There were about 4,500 of them in all. They did no work, but were assigned the job of policing the neighboring Jewish camps and barracks, where they exercised their authority with unimaginable cruelty.

The Gypsy Camp offered one curiosity: the experimental barracks. The director of the Research Laboratory was Dr. Epstein, professor at the University of Prague, a pediatrician of world renown, a KZ prisoner since 1940. His assistant was Dr. Bendel, of the University of Paris Medical School.

Three categories of experiments were performed here:

the first consisted of research into the origin and causes of dual births, a study which the birth of the Dionne quintuplets ten years before had caused to be pursued with renewed interest. The second was the search to discover the biological and pathological causes for the birth of dwarfs and giants. And the third was the study of the causes and treatment of a disease commonly called "dry gangrene of the face."

This terrible disease is exceptionally rare; in ordinary practice you scarcely ever come across it. But here in the Gypsy Camp it was fairly common among both children and adolescents. And so, because of its prevalence, research had been greatly facilitated and considerable progress made towards finding an effective method of treating it.

According to established medical concepts, "dry gangrene of the face" generally appears in conjunction with measles, scarlet fever and typhoid fever. But these diseases, plus the camp's deplorable sanitary conditions, seemed only to be the factors that favored its development, since it also existed in the Czech, Polish and Jewish camps. But it was especially prevalent among gypsy children, and from this it had been deduced that its presence must be directly related to hereditary syphilis, for the syphilis rate in the Gypsy Camp was extremely high.

From these observations a new treatment, consisting of a combination of malaria injections and doses of a drug whose trade name is "Novarsenobenzol," had been developed, with most promising results.

Dr. Mengele paid daily visits to the experimental barracks and participated actively in all phases of the research. He worked in collaboration with two prisoner-doctors and a painter named Dina, whose artistic skill was a great asset to the enterprise. Dina was a native of Prague, and had been a KZ prisoner for three years. As Dr. Mengele's assistant she was granted certain privileges that ordinary prisoners never enjoyed.

5 DR. MENGELE WAS INDEFATIGABLE IN THE exercise of his functions. He spent long hours in his laboratories, then hurried to the unloading platform, where the daily arrival of four or five trainloads of Hungarian deportees kept him busy half the day.

Unceasingly the new convoys marched off in columns of five, flanked by SS guards. I watched one come in and line up. Although my vantage point was at some distance from the tracks and my view obstructed by the maze of barbed wire fences, I could still see that this convoy had been expelled from some fair-sized city: the prisoners' clothes were smartly tailored, many were wearing new poplin raincoats, and the suitcases they carried were of expensive leather. In that city, wherever it was, they had managed to create for themselves a pleasant, cultured way of life. And that was the cardinal sin for which they were now paying so dearly.

Despite his numerous functions, Dr. Mengele even found time for me. A cart, drawn by prisoners, drew up before the dissecting room door. The transportation group unloaded two corpses. On their chests the letters Z and S *(Zur Sektion)*, marked with a special chalk, indicated that they were to be dissected. The chief of Barracks 12 assigned an intelligent prisoner to assist me. Together we placed one of the bodies on the dissection table. I noticed a thick black line across his neck. Either he had hanged himself, or been hanged. Taking a quick look at the second body, I saw that death had here been caused by electrocution. That much could be deduced from the small superficial skin burns and the yellowish-red coloration around them. I wondered whether he had thrown himself against the high-tension wires, or whether he had been pushed. Both were common in the KZ.

The formalities were the same, whether it was a case of suicide or murder. In the evening, at roll call, the

33

names of the deceased would be scratched from the muster list, and their bodies loaded onto "hearses" for transportation to the camp morgue. There another truck would pick them up, at the rate of forty to fifty a day, and bear them to the crematorium.

The two bodies Dr. Mengele had sent me were the first I had been given to examine. The day before, he had warned me to work on them carefully and do a good job. I planned to carry out his orders to the best of my ability.

A car pulled up. In the barracks the command "Attention" rang out. Dr. Mengele and two senior SS officers had just arrived. They listened as the barracks leader and doctor made their reports, then headed straight for the dissecting room, followed by the F Camp prisoner-doctors. They arranged themselves in a circle around the room, as though this were a pathology class in some important medical center and the case at hand a particularly interesting one. I suddenly realized that I was about to take an examination, and that this was the jury before me, a highly important and dangerous jury. I also knew that my fellow prisoner-doctors were keeping their fingers crossed for me.

No one present knew that I had spent three years at the Boroslo Institute of Forensic Medicine, where I had had a chance to study every possible form of suicide under the supervision of Professor Strasseman. I realized that, as prisoner-doctor A 8450, I had better remember now all that Dr. Miklos Nyiszli had formerly known.

I began the dissection. I proceeded to open first the skull, then the thorax and finally the abdominal cavity. I extracted all the organs, noted everything that was abnormal, and replied without hesitation to all the numerous questions they fired at me. Their faces showed that their curiosity had been satisfied, and from their approving nods and glances I surmised that I had passed the examination. After the second dissection Dr. Mengele ordered me to prepare the statement of my findings. Somebody would stop by to pick it up on the following day. After the SS doctors had left I conversed a while with my fellow prisoners.

On the following day three more bodies arrived for dissection. The same public appeared, but this time the atmosphere was less tense, for they knew me and had seen my work. Those present took a more lively interest, made a number of astute and provocative comments, and on certain points the discussion grew quite animated.

After the departure of the SS doctors, several French and Greek doctors paid me a call and asked if I would instruct them in the technique of lumbar punctures. They also requested me to grant them authorization to try the operation on some of the bodies given me, a request I readily granted. I was deeply moved to find that, even inside the barbed wire fences, they continued to manifest such an interest in their profession. They attempted the puncture and after six or seven tries at last succeeded, then withdrew, quite pleased with their afternoon's work.

6 FOR THE NEXT THREE DAYS I HAD NOTHing to do. I was still drawing the supplementary rations issued to doctors, but I spent most of my time either stretched out on my bed or seated on the bleachers of the stadium, which was located not far from F Camp. Yes, even Auschwitz had its stadium. But it was reserved exclusively for the use of the German prisoners of the Third Reich, who acted as clerks in various camp sections. On Sundays the stadium was the excited hub of sports activity, but on weekdays the vast field lay quiet and empty. Only a barbed wire fence separated the stadium from number one crematorium. I wanted very much to know just what went on in the shadow of the immense stack, which never ceased spewing tongues of flame. From where I was sitting there was not much one could see. And to approach the barbed wire was unwise, for the watchtower machine guns sprayed the area without warning to frighten away anyone who happened to wander into this No-Man's-Land.

Nevertheless, I saw that a group of men in civilian clothes was lining up in the crematorium courtyard, directly in front of the red-brick building: there were about 200 in all, with an SS guard in front. It looked to me like a roll call, and I assumed that this was the night watch being relieved by the oncoming day watch. For the crematoriums ran on a twenty-four-hour schedule, as I learned from a fellow prisoner, who also informed me that the crematorium personnel were known as the Sonderkommando, which means, merely, kommandos assigned to special work. They were well fed and given civilian clothes. They were never permitted to leave the grounds of the crematorium, and every four months, when they had learned too much about the place for their own good, they were liquidated. Till now such had been the fate of every Sonderkommando since the founding of the KZ; this explains why no one had ever escaped to tell the world what had been taking place inside these grim walls for the past several years.

I returned to Barracks 12 just in time for Dr. Mengele's arrival. He drove up and was received by the barracks guard, then sent for me and asked me to join him in his car. This time there was no guard with us. We were gone before I even had time to say good-bye to my colleagues. He stopped in front of the Camp Office and asked Dr. Sentkeller to get my card, then started off again along the bumpy road.

For about twelve minutes we drove through the labyrinth of barbed wire and entered well-guarded gates, thus passing from one section to another. Only then did I realize how vast the KZ was. Few people had the possibility of verifying that fact, because the majority died at the very place to which they were sent when they first arrived. Later I learned that the Auschwitz KZ had, at certain periods, held more than 100,000 people within its enclosure of electrified barbed wire.[1]

Dr. Mengele suddenly interrupted my meditations. Without turning, he said: "The place I'm taking you to is no sanatorium, but you'll find that conditions there are not too bad."

We left the camp and skirted the Jewish unloading ramp for about 300 yards. A large armored gate in the barbed wire opened behind the guard. We went in: before us lay a spacious courtyard, covered with green grass. The gravel paths and the shade of the pine trees would have made the place quite pleasant had there not been, at the end of the courtyard, an enormous red brick building

---

[1] Hoess, the camp commander, testified at Nuremberg that the camp held 140,000 prisoners when filled to capacity.—*Tr.*

and a chimney spitting flame. We were in one of the crematoriums. We stayed in the car. An SS ran up and saluted Dr. Mengele. Then we got out, crossed the courtyard and went through a large door into the crematorium.

"Is the room ready?" Dr. Mengele asked the guard.

"Yes, sir," the man replied.

We headed towards it, Dr. Mengele leading the way.

The room in question was freshly whitewashed and well lighted by a large window, which, however, was barred. The furnishings, after those of the barracks, surprised me: a white bed; a closet, also white; a large table and some chairs. On the table, a red velvet tablecloth. The concrete floor was covered with handsome rugs. I had the impression I was expected. The Sonderkommando men had painted the room and outfitted it with objects that the preceding convoys had left behind. We then passed through a dark corridor until we reached another room, a very bright, completely modern dissecting room, with two windows. The floor was of red concrete; in the center of the room, mounted on a concrete base, stood a dissecting table of polished marble, equipped with several drainage channels. At the edge of the table a basin with nickel taps had been installed; against the wall, three porcelain sinks. The walls were painted a light green, and large barred windows were covered with green metal screens to keep out flies and mosquitoes.

We left the dissecting room for the next room: the work room. Here there were fancy chairs and paintings; in the middle of the room, a large table covered with a green cloth; all about, comfortable armchairs. I counted three microscopes on the table. In one corner there was a well-stocked library, which contained the most recent editions. In another corner a closet, in which were stowed white smocks, aprons, towels and rubber gloves. In short, the exact replica of any large city's institute of pathology.

I took it all in, paralyzed with fright. As soon as I had come through the main gate I had realized that I was on death's path. A slow death, opening its maddening depths before me. I felt I was lost.

Now I understood why I had been given civilian clothes. This was the uniform of the Sonderkommando—the kommando of the living-dead.

My chief was preparing to leave; he informed the SS guard that as far as "service" was concerned I depended exclusively on him. The crematorium's SS personnel had no jurisdiction over me. The SS kitchen had to provide my food; I could get my linen and supplementary clothing at the SS warehouse. For shaves and haircuts, I had the right to use the SS barbershop in the building. I would not have to be present for the evening or morning roll call.

Besides my laboratory and anatomical work, I was also responsible for the medical care of all the crematorium's SS personnel—about 120 men—as well as the Sonderkommando—about 860 prisoners. Medicines, medical instruments, dressings, all in sufficient quantity, were at my disposal. So that they should receive suitable medical attention, I had to visit all those sick in the crematorium once a day, and sometimes even twice. I could circulate among the four crematoriums without a pass from 7:00 A.M. till 7:00 P.M. I would have to make out a daily report to the SS commandant and to the Sonderkommando Oberschaarführer Mussfeld, listing the number of ill, bed-ridden and ambulatory patients.

I listened, almost paralyzed, to the enumeration of my rights and duties. Under such conditions, I should be the KZ's most important figure, were I not in the Sonderkommando and were all this not taking place in the "Number one Krema."

Dr. Mengele left without a word. Never did an SS, no matter how low in rank, greet a KZ prisoner. I locked the door to the dissecting room; from now on it was my responsibility.

I returned to my room and sat down, wanting to collect my thoughts. It was not easy. I went back to the beginning. The image of my abandoned home came back to me. I could see the neat little house, with its sunny terraces and pleasant rooms, rooms in which I had spent so many long and trying hours with my patients, but with the satisfaction of knowing I had given them comfort and strength. The same house in which I had spent so many hours of happiness with my family.

We had already been separated for a week. Where could they be, lost in this enormous mass, anonymous, like all those swallowed by this gigantic prison? Had my daughter been able to stay with her mother, or had they already been separated? What had happened to my aged parents, whose last years I had tried to make more pleasant? What had become of my beloved younger sister, whom I had raised practically as my own child after our father had fallen ill? It had been such a pleasure to love and help them. I had no doubt about their fate. They were certainly en route to one of the forty-car trains that would bring them here to the Jewish ramp of the Auschwitz extermination camp. With one mechanical wave of his hand Dr. Mengele would direct my parents into the left-hand column. And my sister would also join that column, for even if she were ordered into the right-hand column, she would surely beg, on bended knee, for permission to go with our mother. So they would let her go, and she, with tears in her eyes, would shower them with thanks.

The news of my arrival had spread like wildfire throughout the crematorium. Both the SS personnel assigned here and the Sonderkommando came to call on me. The door was first opened by an SS noncom. Two extremely tall, militant looking Schaarführer entered. I knew that the attitude I then assumed would determine their conduct towards me in the future. I recalled Dr. Mengele's order: I was responsible only to him. Consequently I considered this visit merely as a private act of courtesy, and remained seated instead of rising and standing at attention. I greeted them and asked them to sit down.

They stopped in the middle of the room and looked me over. I felt the full importance of this moment: it was the first impression that counted. It seemed to me that my manner was the best one to have adopted, for their rigid face muscles relaxed slightly and, with a gesture of careless indifference, they sat down.

The scope of our conversation was extremely limited. How was my trip? What was I doing in the KZ? These were questions they could not ask, for the answers would embarrass them. Whereas politics, the war, and conditions in the KZ were subjects I could not broach. Still, this did not bother me, for the years I had spent in pre-war Germany furnished plenty of material for discussion. They were much impressed by the fact that I spoke their own language better, or at least in a more cultured manner, than they did. I soon realized that there were even certain expressions they did not understand, although they carefully refrained from letting me know it. I knew their country well, was fully informed about life in their cities and their homes, and about their religious and moral concepts. So conversation was not overly difficult for me. I had a feeling that this examination had also been a success, for they left smiling.

More visitors arrived, men in civilian clothes, clean-shaven and smartly dressed. The Kapo-in-chief [1] and two of his men entered my room. This too was a courtesy call. I learned that they were the ones who had had my room prepared. They had heard of my arrival and invited me to dine with them and meet the other prisoners.

As a matter of fact it was almost dinner time. I followed them up the stairs to the second story of the crematorium where the prisoners lived: an enormous room, with comfortable bunks lining both walls. The bunks were made of unpainted wood, but on each one silk coverlets and embroidered pillows shone. This colorful, expensive bedding was completely out of keeping with the atmosphere of the place. It had not been made here, but left by members of earlier convoys who had brought it with them into captivity. The Sonderkommando was allowed to draw it from the storerooms and use it.

The whole room was bathed in a dazzling light, for here they did not economize on electricity as they did in the barracks. Our way led between the long row of bunks. Only half the kommando was present; the other half, about a hundred men, was on the night shift. Some of those here were already in bed asleep, while others were reading. There were plenty of books to be had, for we Jews are a people who like to read. Each prisoner had brought some books with him, the number and type depending upon his level of intelligence and education. To have books and be able to read was yet another privilege granted to the Sonderkommando. In the KZ anyone caught reading was punished with twenty days' solitary confinement, in a sort of sentry box just large enough to stand up in. Unless, of course, the blows dealt him beforehand had already killed him.

The table awaiting us was covered with a heavy silk brocade tablecloth; fine initialled porcelain dishes; and place settings of silver: more objects that had once be-

---

1 Kapo is the abbreviation of *Kamaradschafts Polizei*. The Kapo-in-chief was generally a German prisoner serving a sentence for some non-political crime. A few of them tried to ease the lot of fellow sufferers, but most were faithful servants of the SS.—*Tr.*

longed to the deportees. The table was piled high with choice and varied dishes, everything a deported people could carry with them into the uncertain future: all sorts of preserves, bacon, jellies, several kinds of salami, cakes and chocolate. From the labels I noticed that some of the food had belonged, to Hungarian deportees. All perishable foods automatically became the property of the legal heirs, of those who were still alive, that is, the Sonderkommando.

Seated around the table were the Kapo-in-chief, the engineer, the head chauffeur, the kommando leader, the "tooth pullers" and the head of the gold smelters. Their welcome was most cordial. They offered me all they had, and there was an abundance of everything, for the Hungarian convoys continued to arrive at an ever-increasing rate and they brought a great deal of food with them.

I found it difficult to swallow, however. I could not help thinking of my fellow-sufferers who, before starting on their exodus, had gathered and prepared their provisions. They had been hungry, but had refrained from eating during the entire trip in order to save their meager rations for their parents, their children and the more difficult times ahead. Only the more difficult times had never come: in the lobby of the crematorium the food had remained untouched.

I drank some tea spiked with rum. After a few glasses I managed to relax. My mind cleared and freed itself of the unpleasant thoughts that had been plaguing it. A pleasant warmth penetrated me: the voluptuous effects of the alcohol, comforting as the caress of a mother's hand.

The cigarettes we were smoking had also been "Imported from Hungary." In the camp proper a single cigarette was worth a ration of bread: here on the table lay hundreds of packages.

Our conversation grew more and more spirited. Poland, France, Greece, Germany and Italy were represented around the table. Since most of us understood German it served as our common language. From the conversation I learned the history of the crematoriums. Tens of thousands of prisoners had built them of stone and concrete, finishing them in the middle of an extremely rigorous winter. Every stone was stained with their blood. They had worked day and night, often without food or drink, dressed in mere tatters, so that these infernal death-factories, whose first victims they became, might be finished in time.

Since then four years had passed. Countless thousands had since climbed down from the box cars and crossed the threshold of the crematoriums. The present Sonderkommando was the twelfth to bear the name. I learned the history of each preceding Sonderkommando, when it "reigned" and who its heroes were, and I was reminded of a fact I already knew: that the Sonderkommando's life span was only a few months at the most.

Whoever among them practiced the Jewish faith could thus begin, on the day of his arrival, the purification ceremony in preparation for death. For death would come to him as surely as it had come to every member of all the preceding Sonderkommandos.

It was almost midnight. The company assembled around the table was weary from the day's work and the evening's consumption of alcohol. Our conversation grew more and more listless. An SS making his rounds stopped to remind us that it was high time we were in bed. I took leave of my new companions and returned to my room. Thanks to the rum I had drunk and my tired nerves, I spent a relatively quiet first night.

7 THE STRIDENT WHISTLE OF A TRAIN WAS heard coming from the direction of the unloading platform. It was still very early. I approached my window, from which I had a direct view onto the tracks, and saw a very long train. A few seconds later the doors slid open and the box cars spilled out thousands upon thousands of the chosen people of Israel. Line up and selection took scarcely half an hour. The left-hand column moved slowly away.

Orders rang out, and the sounds of rapid footsteps reached my room. The sounds came from the furnace rooms of the crematorium: they were preparing to welcome the new convoy. The throb of motors began. They had just set the enormous ventilators going to fan the flames, in order to obtain the desired degree in the ovens. Fifteen ventilators were going simultaneously, one beside each oven. The incineration room was about 500 feet long: it was a bright, whitewashed room with a concrete floor and barred windows. Each of these fifteen ovens was housed in a red brick structure. Immense iron doors, well-polished and gleaming, ominously lined the length of the wall. In five or six minutes the convoy reached the gate, whose swing-doors opened inwards. Five abreast, the group entered the courtyard; it was the moment about which the outside world knew nothing, for anyone who might have known something about it, after having traveled the path of his destiny—the 300 yards separating that spot from the ramp—had never returned to tell the tale. It was one of the crematoriums which awaited those who had been selected for the left-hand column. And not, as the German lie had made the right-hand column suppose in order to allay their anxiety, a camp for the sick and children, where the infirm cared for the little ones.

They advanced with slow, weary steps. The children's eyes were heavy with sleep and they clung to their mother's clothes. For the most part the babies were carried in their fathers' arms, or else wheeled in their carriages. The SS guards remained before the crematorium doors, where a poster announced: "Entrance is Strictly Forbidden to All Who Have No Business Here, Including SS."

The deportees were quick to notice the water faucets, used for sprinkling the grass, that were arranged about the courtyard. They began to take pots and pans from their luggage, and broke ranks, pushing and shoving in an effort to get near the faucets and fill their containers. That they were impatient was not astonishing: for the past five days they had had nothing to drink. If ever they had found a little water, it had been stagnant and had not quenched their thirst. The SS guards who received the convoys were used to the scene. They waited patiently till each had quenched his thirst and filled his container. In any case, the guards knew that as long as they had not drunk there would be no getting them back into line. Slowly they began to re-form their ranks. Then they advanced for about 100 yards along a cinder path edged with green grass to an iron ramp, from which 10 or 12 concrete steps led underground to an enormous room dominated by a large sign in German, French, Greek and Hungarian: "Baths and Disinfecting Room." The sign was reassuring, and allayed the misgivings or fears of even the most suspicious among them. They went down the stairs almost gaily.

The room into which the convoy proceeded was about 200 yards long: its walls were whitewashed and it was brightly lit. In the middle of the room, rows of columns. Around the columns, as well as along the walls, benches. Above the benches, numbered coat hangers. Numerous signs in several languages drew everyone's attention to the necessity of tying his clothes and shoes together. Especially that he not forget the number of his coat hanger, in order to avoid all useless confusion upon his return from the bath.

"That's really a German order," commented those who had long been inclined to admire the Germans.

They were right. As a matter of fact, it *was* for the sake of order that these measures had been taken, so that the thousands of pairs of good shoes sorely needed by the Third Reich would not get mixed up. The same for the clothes, so that the population of bombed cities could easily make use of them.

There were 3,000 people in the room: men, women and children. Some of the soldiers arrived and announced that everyone must be completely undressed within ten minutes. The aged, grandfathers and grandmothers; the children; wives and husbands; all were struck dumb with surprise. Modest women and girls looked at each other questioningly. Perhaps they had not exactly understood the German words. They did not have long to think about it, however, for the order resounded again, this time in a louder, more menacing tone. They were uneasy; their dignity rebelled; but, with the resignation peculiar to their race, having learned that anything went as far they were concerned, they slowly began to undress. The aged, the paralyzed, the mad were helped by a Sonderkommando squad sent for that purpose. In ten minutes all were completely naked, their clothes hung on the pegs, their shoes attached together by the laces. As for the number of each clothes hanger, it had been carefully noted.

Making his way through the crowd, an SS opened the swing-doors of the large oaken gate at the end of the room. The crowd flowed through it into another, equally well-lighted room. This second room was the same size as the first, but neither benches nor pegs were to be seen. In the center of the rooms, at thirty-yard intervals, columns rose from the concrete floor to the ceiling. They were not supporting columns, but square sheet-iron pipes, the sides of which contained numerous perforations, like a wire lattice.

Everyone was inside. A hoarse command rang out: "SS and Sonderkommando leave the room." They obeyed and counted off. The doors swung shut and from without the lights were switched off.

At that very instant the sound of a car was heard: a deluxe model, furnished by the International Red Cross. An SS officer and a SDG (*Santätsdienstgefreiter:* Deputy Health Service Officer) stepped out of the car. The Deputy Health Officer held four green sheet-iron canisters. He advanced across the grass, where, every thirty yards, short concrete pipes jutted up from the ground. Having donned his gas mask, he lifted the lid of the pipe, which was also made of concrete. He opened one of the cans and poured the contents—a mauve granulated material—into the opening. The granulated substance fell in a lump to the bottom. The gas it produced escaped through the perforations, and within a few seconds filled the room in which the deportees were stacked. Within five minutes everybody was dead.

For every convoy it was the same story. Red Cross cars brought the gas from the outside. There was never a stock of it in the crematorium. The precaution was scandalous, but still more scandalous was the fact that the gas was brought in a car bearing the insignia of the International Red Cross.

In order to be certain of their business the two gas-butchers waited another five minutes. Then they lighted cigarettes and drove off in their car. They had just killed 3,000 innocents.

Twenty minutes later the electric ventilators were set going in order to evacuate the gas. The doors opened, the trucks arrived, and a Sonderkommando squad loaded the clothing and the shoes separately. They were going to disinfect them. This time it was a case of real disinfection. Later they would transport them by rail to various parts of the country.

The ventilators, patented "Exhator" system, quickly evacuated the gas from the room, but in the crannies between the dead and the cracks of the doors small pockets of it always remained. Even two hours later it caused a suffocating cough. For that reason the Sonderkommando group which first moved into the room was equipped with gas masks. Once again the room was powerfully lighted, revealing a horrible spectacle.

The bodies were not lying here and there throughout the room, but piled in a mass to the ceiling. The reason for this was that the gas first inundated the lower layers of air and rose but slowly towards the ceiling. This forced the victims to trample one another in a frantic effort to escape the gas. Yet a few feet higher up the gas reached them. What a struggle for life there must have been! Nevertheless it was merely a matter of two or three minutes' respite. If they had been able to think about what they were doing, they would have realized they were trampling their own children, their wives, their relatives. But they couldn't think. Their gestures were no more than the reflexes of the instinct of self-preservation. I noticed that the bodies of the women, the children, and the aged were at the bottom of the pile; at the top, the strongest. Their bodies, which were covered with scratches and bruises from the struggle which had set them against each other, were often interlaced. Blood oozed from their noses and mouths; their faces, bloated and blue, were so deformed as to be almost unrecognizable. Nevertheless some of the Sonderkommando often did recognize their kin. The encounter was not easy, and I dreaded it for myself. I had no reason to be here, and yet I had come down among the dead. I felt it my duty to my people and to the entire world to be able to give an accurate account of what I had seen if ever, by some miraculous whim of fate, I should escape.

The Sonderkommando squad, outfitted with large rubber boots, lined up around the hill of bodies and flooded it with powerful jets of water. This was necessary because the final act of those who die by drowning or by gas is an involuntary defecation. Each body was befouled, and had to be washed. Once the "bathing" of the dead was finished—a job the Sonderkommando carried out by a voluntary act of impersonalization and in a state of profound distress—the separation of the welter of bodies began. It was a difficult job. They knotted thongs around the wrists, which were clenched in a viselike grip, and with these thongs they dragged the slippery bodies to the elevators in the next room. Four good-sized elevators were functioning. They loaded twenty to twenty-five corpses to an elevator. The ring of a bell was the signal that the load was ready to ascend. The elevator stopped at the crematorium's incineration room, where large sliding doors opened automatically. The kommando who operated the trailers was ready and waiting. Again straps were fixed to the wrists of the dead, and they were dragged onto specially constructed chutes which unloaded them in front of the furnaces.

The bodies lay in close ranks: the old, the young, the children. Blood oozed from their noses and mouths, as well as from their skin—abraded by the rubbing—and mixed with the water running in the gutters set in the concrete floor.

Then a new phase of the exploitation and utilization of Jewish bodies took place. The Third Reich had already taken their clothes and shoes. Hair was also a precious material, due to the fact that it expands and contracts uniformly, no matter what the humidity of the air. Human hair was often used in delayed action bombs, where its particular qualities made it highly useful for detonating purposes. So they shaved the dead.

But that was not all. According to the slogans the Germans paraded and shouted to everyone at home and abroad, the Third Reich was not based on the "gold standard," but on the "work standard." Maybe they meant they had to work harder to get their gold than most countries did. At any rate, the dead were next sent to the "tooth-pulling" kommando, which was stationed in front of the ovens. Consisting of eight men, this kommando equipped its members with two tools, or, if you like, two instruments. In one hand a lever, and in the other a pair of pliers for extracting the teeth. The dead lay on their backs; the kommando pried open the contracted jaw with his lever; then, with his pliers, he extracted, or broke off, all gold teeth, as well as any gold bridgework and fillings. All members of the kommando were fine stomatologists and dental surgeons. When Dr. Mengele had called for candidates capable of performing the delicate work of stomatology and dental surgery, they had volunteered in good faith, firmly believing they would be allowed to exercise their profession in the camp. Exactly as I had done.

The gold teeth were collected in buckets filled with an acid which burned off all pieces of bone and flesh. Other valuables worn by the dead, such as necklaces, pearls, wedding bands and rings, were taken and dropped through a slot in the lid of a strongbox. Gold is a heavy metal, and I would judge that from 18 to 20 pounds of it were collected daily in each crematorium. It varied, to be sure, from one convoy to the next, for some convoys were comparatively wealthy, while others, from rural districts, were naturally poorer.

The Hungarian convoys arrived already stripped. But the Dutch, Czech, and Polish convoys, even after several years in the ghettos, had managed to keep and bring their jewelry, their gold and their dollars with them. In this way the Germans amassed considerable treasures.

When the last gold tooth had been removed, the bodies went to the incineration kommando. There they were laid by threes on a kind of pushcart made of sheet metal. The heavy doors of the ovens opened automatically; the pushcart moved into a furnace heated to incandescence.

The bodies were cremated in twenty minutes. Each crematorium worked with fifteen ovens, and there were four crematoriums. This meant that several thousand people could be cremated in a single day. Thus for weeks and months—even years—several thousand people passed each day through the gas chambers and from there to the incineration ovens. Nothing but a pile of ashes remained in the crematory ovens. Trucks took the ashes to the Vistula, a mile away, and dumped them into the raging waters of the river.

After so much suffering and horror there was still no peace, even for the dead.

8 THE LABORATORY OF PATHOLOGY WAS SET up at the instigation of my superior, Dr. Mengele, and was destined to satisfy his ambitions in the area of medical research. It had been completed only a few days before. All that was needed for it to start functioning was a doctor capable of taking charge.

The confines of the KZ offered vast possibilities for research, first in the field of forensic medicine, because of the high suicide rate, and also in the field of pathology, because of the relatively high percentage of dwarfs, giants and other abnormal types of human beings. The abundance—unequaled elsewhere in the world—of corpses, and the fact that one could dispose of them freely for purposes of research, opened even wider horizons.

I knew from experience that, whereas the clinics in most major cities of the world managed to furnish their institutes of forensic medicine with from 100 to 150 bodies for purposes of research, the Auschwitz KZ was capable of furnishing literally millions. Any person who had entered the gates of the KZ was a candidate for death. He whose destiny had directed him into the left-hand column was transformed by the gas chambers into a corpse within an hour after his arrival. Less fortunate was he whom adversity had singled out for the right-hand column. He was still a candidate for death, but with this difference, that for three or four months, or as long as he could endure, he had to submit to all the horrors the KZ had to offer, till he dropped from utter exhaustion. He bled from a thousand wounds. His belly was contorted with hunger, his eyes were haggard, and he moaned like one demented. He dragged his body across the fields of snow till he could go no farther. Trained dogs snapped at his wretched, fleshless frame, and when even the lice forsook his desiccated body, then the hour of deliverance, the hour of redeeming death was close at hand. Who then—of our parents, brothers, children —was more fortunate, he who went to the left or he who went to the right?

When the convoys arrived, soldiers scouted the ranks lined up before the box cars, hunting for twins and dwarfs. Mothers, hoping for special treatment for their twin children, readily gave them up to the scouts. Adult twins, knowing that they were of interest from a scientific point of view, voluntarily presented themselves, in the hope of better treatment. The same for dwarfs.

They were separated from the rest and herded to the right. They were allowed to keep their civilian clothes; guards accompanied them to specially designed barracks, where they were treated with a certain regard. Their food was good, their bunks were comfortable, and possibilities for hygiene were provided.

They were housed in Barracks 14 of Camp F. From there they were taken by their guards to the experimentation barracks of the Gypsy Camp, and exposed to every medical examination that can be performed on human beings: blood tests, lumbar punctures, exchanges of blood between twin brothers, as well as numerous other examinations, all fatiguing and depressing. Dina, the painter from Prague, made the comparative studies of the structure of the twins' skulls, ears, noses, mouths, hands and feet. Each drawing was classified in a file set up for that express purpose, complete with all individual characteristics; into this file would also go the final results of this research. The procedure was the same for the dwarfs.

The experiments, in medical language called *in vivo*, *i.e.*, experiments performed on live human beings, were far from exhausting the research possibilities in the study of twins. Full of lacunae, they offered no better than partial results. The *in vivo* experiments were succeeded by the most important phase of twin-study: the comparative examination from the viewpoints of anatomy and pathology. Here it was a question of comparing the twins' healthy organs with those functioning abnormally, or of comparing their illnesses. For that study, as for all studies of a pathological nature, corpses were needed. Since it was necessary to perform a dissection for the simultaneous evaluation of anomalies, the twins had to

die at the same time. So it was that they met their death
in the B section of one of Auschwitz's KZ barracks, at
the hand of Dr. Mengele.

This phenomenon was unique in world medical science
history. Twin brothers died together, and it was possible
to perform autopsies on both. Where, under normal circumstances, can one find twin brothers who die at the
same place and at the same time? For twins, like everyone else, are separated by life's varying circumstances.
They live far from each other and almost never die
simultaneously. One may die at the age of ten, the other
at fifty. Under such conditions comparative dissection
is impossible. In the Auschwitz camp, however, there
were several hundred sets of twins, and therefore as many
possibilities of dissection. That was why, on the arrival
platform, Dr. Mengele separated twins and dwarfs from
the other prisoners. That was why both special groups
were directed to the right-hand column, and thence to
the barracks of the spared. That was why they had good
food and hygienic living conditions, so that they didn't
contaminate each other and die one before the other.
They had to die together, and in good health.

The Sonderkommando chief came hunting for me and
announced that an SS soldier was waiting for me at
the door of the crematorium with a crew of corpse-
transporting kommandos. I went in search of them, for
they were forbidden to enter the courtyard. I took the
documents concerning the corpses from the hands of the
SS. They contained files on two little twin brothers. The
kommando crew, made up entirely of women, set the
covered coffin down in front of me. I lifted the lid. Inside
lay a set of two-year-old twins. I ordered two of my men
to take the corpses and place them on the dissecting table.

I opened the file and glanced through it. Very detailed
clinical examinations, accompanied by X-rays, descriptions, and artists' drawings, indicating from the scientific
viewpoint the different aspects of these two little beings'
"twinhood." Only the pathological report was missing.
It was my job to supply it. The twins had died at the same
time and were now lying beside each other on the big dissecting table. It was they who had to—or whose tiny
bodies had to—resolve the secret of the reproduction of
the race. To advance one step in the search to unlock

the secret of multiplying the race of superior beings destined to rule was a "noble goal." If only it were possible, in the future, to have each German mother bear as many twins as possible! The project, conceived by the demented theorists of the Third Reich, was utterly mad. And it was to Dr. Mengele, chief physician of the Auschwitz KZ, the notorious "criminal doctor," that these experiments had been entrusted.

Among malefactors and criminals, the most dangerous type is the "criminal doctor," especially when he is armed with powers such as those granted to Dr. Mengele. He sent millions of people to death merely because, according to a racial theory, they were inferior beings and therefore detrimental to mankind. This same criminal doctor spent long hours beside me, either at his microscopes, his disinfecting ovens and his test tubes or, standing with equal patience near the dissecting table, his smock befouled with blood, his bloody hands examining and experimenting like one possessed. The immediate objective was the increased reproduction of the German race. The final objective was the production of pure Germans in numbers sufficient to replace the Czechs, Hungarians, Poles, all of whom were condemned to be destroyed, but who for the moment were living on those territories declared vital to the Third Reich.

I finished the dissection of the little twins and wrote out a regulation report of the dissection. I did my job well and my chief appeared to be satisfied with me. But he had some trouble reading my handwriting, for all my letters were capitals, a habit I had picked up in America.[1] And so I told him that if he wanted clear clean copy, he would have to supply me with a typewriter, since I was accustomed to work with one in my own practice.

"What make typewriter are you used to?" he asked.

"Olympia Elite," I said.

"Very well, I'll send you one. You'll have it tomorrow. I want clean copy, because these reports will be forwarded to the Institute of Biological, Racial and Evolu-

[1] Dr. Nyiszli came to the United States in the summer of 1939, and remained until February of 1940, as a member of the Rumanian delegation to the World's Fair. He had intended to bring his family over and settle in America. But during his stay war broke out and he returned to his family. Once back, it was impossible for him to leave the country again. As a result, Auschwitz.—*Tr.*

tionary Research at Berlin-Dahlem."

Thus I learned that the experiments performed here were checked by the highest medical authorities at one of the most famous scientific institutes in the world.

The following day an SS soldier brought me an "Olympia" typewriter. Still more corpses of twins were sent to me. They delivered me four pairs from the Gypsy Camp; all four were under ten years old.

I began the dissection of one set of twins and recorded each phase of my work. I removed the brain pan. Together with the cerebellum I extracted the brain and examined them. Then followed the opening of the thorax and the removal of the sternum. Next I separated the tongue by means of an incision made beneath the chin. With the tongue came the esophagus, with the respiratory tracts came both lungs. I washed the organs in order to examine them more thoroughly. The tiniest spot or the slightest difference in color could furnish valuable information. I made a transverse incision across the pericardium and removed the fluid. Next I took out the heart and washed it. I turned it over and over in my hand to examine it.

In the exterior coat of the left ventricle was a small pale red spot caused by a hypodermic injection, which scarcely differed from the color of the tissue around it. There could be no mistake. The injection had been given with a very small needle. Without a doubt a hypodermic needle. For what purpose had he received the injection? Injections into the heart can be administered in extremely serious cases, when the heart begins to fail. I would soon know. I opened the heart, starting with the ventricle. Normally the blood contained in the left ventricle is taken out and weighed. This method could not be employed in the present case, because the blood was coagulated into a compact mass. I extracted the coagulum with the forceps and brought it to my nose. I was struck by the characteristic odor of chloroform. The victim had received an injection of chloroform in the heart, so that the blood of the ventricle, in coagulating, would deposit on the valves and cause instantaneous death by heart failure.

My discovery of the most monstrous secret of the Third Reich's medical science made my knees tremble. Not only did they kill with gas, but also with injections of chloroform into the heart. A cold sweat broke out on my forehead. Luckily I was alone. If others had been present it would have been difficult for me to conceal my excitement. I finished the dissection, noted the differences found, and recorded them. But the chloroform, the blood coagulated in the left ventricle, the puncture visible in the external coat of the heart, did not figure among my findings. It was a useful precaution on my part. Dr. Mengele's records on the subject of twins were in my hands. They contained the exact examinations, X-rays, the artist's sketches already mentioned, but neither the circumstances nor causes of death. Nor did I fill out that column of the dissection report. It was not a good idea to exceed the authorized bounds of knowledge or to relate all one had witnessed. And here still less than anywhere else. I was not timorous by nature and my nerves were good. During my medical practice I had often brought to light the causes of death. I had seen the bodies of people assassinated for motives of revenge, jealousy, or material gain, as well those of suicides and natural deaths. I was used to the study of well-hidden causes of death. On several occasions I had been shocked by my discoveries, but now a shudder of fear ran through me. If Dr. Mengele had any idea that I had discovered the secret of his injections he would send ten doctors, in the name of the political SS, to attest to my death.

In accordance with orders received I returned the corpses to the prisoners whose duty it was to burn them. They performed their job without delay. I had to keep any organs of possible scientific interest, so that Dr. Mengele could examine them. Those which might interest the Anthropological Institute at Berlin-Dahlem were preserved in alcohol. These parts were specially packed to be sent through the mails. Stamped "War Material—Urgent," they were given top priority in transit. In the course of my work at the crematorium I dispatched an impressive number of such packages. I received, in reply, either precise scientific observations or instructions. In order to classify this correspondence I had to set up special files. The directors of the Berlin-Dahlem Institute always warmly thanked Dr. Mengele for this rare and precious material.

I finished dissecting the three other pairs of twins and duly recorded the anomalies found. In all three instances

the cause of death was the same: an injection of chloroform into the heart.

Of the four sets of twins, three had ocular globes of
different colors. One eye was brown, the other blue. This
is a phenomenon found fairly frequently in non-twins.
But in the present case I noticed that it had occurred in
six out of the eight twins. An extremely interesting collection of anomalies. Medical science calls them hetero-
chromes, which means, merely, different-colored. I cut
out the eyes and put them in a solution of formaldehyde,
noting their characteristics exactly, in order not to mix
them up. During my examination of the four sets of twins,
I discovered still another curious phenomenon: while
removing the skin from the neck I noticed, just above
the upper extremity of the sternum, a tumor about the
size of a small nut. Pressing on it with my forceps I
found it to be filled with a thick pus. This rare manifestation, well known to medical science, indicates the presence
of hereditary syphilis and is called DuBois' tumor. Looking farther, I found that it existed in all eight twins. I
cut out the tumor, leaving it surrounded by healthy tissue, and placed it in another jar of formaldehyde. In
two sets of twins I also discovered evidence of active,
cavernous tuberculosis. I recorded my findings on the dissection report, but left the heading "Cause of Death"
blank.

During the afternoon Dr. Mengele paid me a visit. I
gave him a detailed account of my morning's work and
handed him my report. He sat down and began to read
each case carefully. He was greatly interested by the
heterochromatic condition of the eyes, but even more so
by the discovery of DuBois' tumor. He gave me instructions to have the organs mailed and told me to include
my report in the package. He also instructed me to fill out
the "Cause of Death" column hitherto left blank. The
choice of causes was left to my own judgment and discretion; the only stipulation was that each cause be different. Almost apologetically he remarked that, as I
could see for myself, these children were syphilitic and
tubercular, and consequently would not have lived in
any case . . . He said no more about it. With that he had
said enough. He had explained the reason for these children's death. I had refrained from making any comment.
But I had learned that here tuberculosis and syphilis were

not treated with medicines and drugs, but with chloroform injections.

I shuddered to think of all I had learned during my short stay here, and of all I should yet have to witness without protesting, until my own appointed hour arrived. The minute I entered this place I had the feeling I was already one of the living-dead. But now, in possession of all these fantastic secrets, I was certain I would never get out alive. Was it conceivable that Dr. Mengele, or the Berlin-Dahlem Institute, would ever allow me to leave this place alive?

9 IT WAS ALREADY LATE, AND GROWING DARK. Dr. Mengele had left and I was alone with my thoughts. Mechanically I arranged the instruments used for the autopsy and, after washing my hands, went into the work room and lighted a cigarette, hoping to find a minute's peace. Suddenly I heard a scream that sent chills up and down my spine. Then, immediately afterwards, a thud that sounded like a falling body. I listened, my nerves taut, for what the following minutes would bring. Before another minute had passed I heard another scream, a click and the fall of a body. I counted seventy screams, clicks, thuds. Heavy footsteps retreated and all grew quiet.

The scene of the bloody tragedy that had just been enacted was the room adjoining the dissecting room. The hall led directly into it. It was a half-darkened place, with a concrete floor and barred windows that looked out onto the back courtyard. I used it as a storeroom for corpses, keeping them there till it was their turn for dissection, then returning them there after the autopsy till they were sent to be burned. Used, dirty, women's clothes; battered wooden shoes; glasses; pieces of stale bread—the normal run of KZ women's articles—lay piled before the entrance to the room. After what I had heard I was prepared for something extraordinary. I entered the room and glanced quickly around. A terrifying scene gradually unfolded: before me were sprawled the naked bodies of seventy women; curled up, bathed in their own blood and in the blood of their neighbors, they lay in utter disarray about the room.

As my eyes grew more accustomed to the dim light I discovered to my horror that not all the victims were dead. Some were still breathing, moving their arms or legs slowly; with glazed eyes, they tried to raise their bloody heads. I lifted two, three heads of those still alive, and suddenly realized that, besides death by gas and chloroform injections, there was a third way of killing here: a bullet in the back of the neck. The wound revealed that a six-millimeter bullet had been used: there was no exit hole. From these cursory observations, I concluded that it had been a soft lead bullet, because only this type bullet will imbed itself in the skull structure. Unfortunately I knew something of such matters and was able to size up the situation quickly in all its horror. There was nothing surprising in the fact that these small-caliber bullets did not cause instantaneous death in all cases, although they were fired—the powder burns on the skin proved it—from a distance of only an inch or two, right into the spinal medulla. It appeared that in some instances the bullet had deviated slightly from its path; thus death had not always been instantaneous.

I took note of that as well, but meditated no further; I was afraid of going mad. Stepping out into the courtyard I asked a member of the Sonderkommando where the women had come from.

"They were taken from C Section," he said. "Every evening a truck brings seventy of them. They all get a bullet in the back of the neck."

My head spinning, struck dumb with horror, I walked along the gravel path which divided the well-kept lawn of the crematorium courtyard. My gaze wandered to the evening muster of Sonderkommando. This evening there was no change of guard. Number one crematorium was not working today. I glanced in the direction of numbers two, three and four: their chimneys were spewing flame and smoke. Business as usual.

It was too early for dinner. The Sonderkommando brought out a football. The teams lined up on the field.

"SS versus SK." On one side of the field the crematorium's SS guards; on the other, the Sonderkommando. They put the ball into play. Sonorous laughter filled the courtyard. The spectators became excited and shouted encouragement at the players, as if this were the playing field of some peaceful town. Stupefied, I made that mental note as well. Without waiting for the end of the match, I returned to my room. After supper I swallowed two sleeping tablets of ten centigrams each and fell asleep. A badly needed sleep, for I felt my nerves stretched to the breaking point. In such cases, sleeping tablets were the best remedy.

10 IN THE MORNING I AWOKE WITH A HANG-over. I crossed to the shower which had been set up in a neighboring room and let the icy waters of the Vistula splash over me for half an hour. It refreshed my tired nerves and chased the heaviness caused by the sleeping pills.

How well the Germans cared for us! They had built a beautiful ten-man shower, made of gleaming tile, for the exclusive use of the Sonderkommando members. Those who worked with corpses had to wash frequently, so showers were mandatory twice a day, a regulation to which we all gladly submitted.

I checked the contents of my medical bag. It had been brought to me from the storeroom by a Sonder man and had probably belonged to one of my medical colleagues, who had checked it with his clothes in the cloakroom before entering the gas chamber. In it I found a stethoscope, an apparatus for taking blood pressure, some good syringes, a number of other essential instruments and drugs, and several ampoules for emergency injections. I was happy to have it, for I knew that it would come in handy during my "visits." Here, in the Sonderkommando, "visits" meant making the rounds of the four crematoriums.

I began with my own building. First I stopped at the SS living quarters, planning to examine anyone who showed up, for there were always a few. In the crematoriums everyone feigned illness from time to time in order to get a short respite from his exhausting and nerve-racking labors. There were also more serious cases upon occasion, but we had no trouble taking care of them: as for medical supplies, we could have vied with the best-stocked drugstore in Berlin.

A special kommando was given the job of inspecting the luggage left in the gas chamber lobbies and recouping all medicines before the clothes and shoes were shipped away. These medicines were then turned over to me to be arranged and classified according to their type and purpose. It was no easy job, for people were brought to Auschwitz from all over Europe, and the medicines they brought with them were naturally labeled in the language of the country of origin. So I found labels written in Greek, Polish, Czech and Dutch, all of which I had to decipher. I might mention in passing that the majority of medicines found on those who had been brought to the KZ belonged to one of several kinds of sedatives. Sedatives to quiet the nerves of Europe's persecuted Jews.

Following my visit to the SS, I proceeded upstairs to the Sonderkommando's living quarters. While I was there I treated a few cuts and bruises, common among chauffeurs. The Sonderkommando men seldom had any organic illnesses, for their clothes were clean, their beds were provided with fresh linen, and their food was good, sometimes even excellent. Besides they were all young men, hand-picked for their strength and good physical constitution. They did have, however, a general tendency to nervous disorders, for it was a tremendous strain on them to know that their brothers, their wives, their parents—their entire race—were perishing here. Day after day they took thousands of corpses and dragged them to the crematory ovens, where they loaded them with their own hands into the incineration cases. The result was acute nervous depression, and often neurasthenia. Everybody here had a past which he looked back on with sorrow, and a future he contemplated with despair. The Sonderkommando's future was tightly circumscribed by time. Four years' painful experience had shown that its life span was four months. At the end of that period a company of SS appeared. The entire kommando was herded into the crematorium's rear courtyard. A machine-gun blast. Half an hour later a new Sonderkommando squad arrived. They undressed their dead companions. An hour later only a heap of ashes remained. The first job of every Sonderkommando crew was the cremation of its predecessor. During my visits there was always someone who took me aside and begged me to give him a swift, sure poison. I invariably refused. Today I am sorry I did. They are all dead. Their death was swift and sure all right—not self-administered as they would have preferred, but at the hands of the Nazi butchers.

11 MY NEXT VISIT TOOK ME TO NUMBER TWO crematorium, which was separated from number one by a path through some fields and by the Jewish unloading platform along the railroad tracks. It was built according to the same plans as number one. The only difference I noticed was that the space corresponding to the dissection room in number one was here used as a gold foundry. Otherwise the layout of the undressing room, the gas chamber, the incineration room and the living quarters of the SS and the Sonderkommando was exactly the same.

It was to the foundry that all the gold teeth and bridgework collected in the four crematoriums were brought, all the jewelry and gold coins, the precious stones and platinum objects, the watches, the gold cigarette cases and any other precious metal found in the trunks, the suitcases, the clothes, or on the bodies of the dead. Three goldsmiths were employed here. First they disinfected the jewelry, then sorted and classified it. They removed the precious stones and sent the settings to the foundry. The gold teeth and jewelry supplied each day by the four crematoriums produced, once smelted, between 65 and 75 pounds of pure gold.

The smelting took place in a graphite crucible about two inches in diameter. The weight of the gold cylinder was 140 grams. I knew that figure to be exact because I had weighed more than one an accurate scale in the dissecting room.

The doctors who removed the teeth from the bodies prior to cremation did not throw all the precious metal into the bucket filled with acid, for a portion—sometimes a fair amount, sometimes only a little—went into the pockets of the SS guards when these morbid treasures were being collected. It was the same for the jewelry and gems sewed into the linings of the clothes, and the gold coins left in the undressing room. In the latter instance, however, it was the Sonderkommando entrusted with the job of going through the luggage who profited. An exceedingly dangerous game, though, for the SS guards were ubiquitous, and they kept a close watch on this newly acquired property, which henceforth belonged to the Third Reich. Needless to say, they kept an especially close watch on the gold and jewelry.

At first I did not understand how, from a judicial or moral point of view, the Sonderkommando could bring themselves to pocket the gold. But a few days later, once I had a better grasp of the situation, I was inclined to agree that it was indeed the Sonderkommando who should—if anybody should—be considered the sole heirs and legal proprietors of the treasures which fortune had brought their way.

The men of the Sonderkommando also turned their gold over to be smelted. Despite the strictest supervision there were always ways of getting it to the goldsmiths and of later retrieving it in the form of 140 gram "coins." But putting this gold to work, that is, exchanging it for useful goods, was a more difficult job. No one dreamed of hoarding his gold, for he knew that in four months' time he would be dead. But for us four months was a very long time. To be condemned to death and yet forced to perform jobs such as we had to perform day after day was enough to break the body and soul of the strongest among us, and to drive many to the brink of insanity. It was thus necessary to make life easier, more bearable, even for a few weeks' time. With gold you could do that, even in the crematoriums.

Thus was born, in the days of the first Sonderkommando, a unit of exchange: the 140 gram gold cylinder. This same unit was still being used by the twelfth Sonderkommando. The goldsmiths did not have any crucible of a smaller diameter, so there was no way for them to make a smaller "coin."

In the crematoriums an object had no "value" in the ordinary sense of the term. Anyone who paid for something with gold had already paid with his life the day he entered here. But the person who gave something in exchange for gold doubly risked his neck, once when he brought the articles that were hard to come by, even on the outside, through the SS barricades and check points, and again on his return trip carrying the gold he had received in payment. For, both coming in and leaving, one was always searched.

On its way out the gold was carried in a Sonderkommando man's pocket as far as the crematorium gate. There it changed hands. The man carrying the gold approached the SS guard on duty and exchanged a few words with him. The latter turned and sauntered away from the gate. On the section of railway track that passed in front of the "Krema" a team of from 20 to 25 Poles was working. At a sign from the Sonderkommando man, their work boss arrived with a folded sack and took the gold, which was wrapped in paper. So the sack containing the desired articles was safely inside the crematorium.

The Sonderkommando man entered the guardhouse, which was near the gate. He took about a hundred cigarettes and a bottle of brandy from the sack. The SS trooper entered and quickly pocketed both the bottle and cigarettes. He was of course extremely pleased, for the SS received only two cigarettes a day and no alcohol at all. And yet both were indispensable here. The SS guards drank and smoked heavily; so did the Sonderkommando.

Other necessary items, such as butter, eggs, ham and onions, were smuggled in by this same method. Nothing of this sort arrived with the deportees. Since the gold was procured through a collective effort, the distribution of the merchandise received in exchange was made on this same basis. Thus both the crematorium personnel and the SS non-coms received an ample supply of food, liquor and cigarettes. Everyone shut his eyes to this traf-

fic, for it was to everyone's advantage that it continue.
Taken individually, any SS guard in the crematorium
could be bought. They distrusted only themselves, knowing that the Sonderkommando had never betrayed anyone and never would. That was why the food, liquor
and cigarettes were turned over to one SS guard by one
"confidence man" from the kommando.

By this same underground route the official organ
of the Third Reich, the *Völkischer Beobachter* was
brought every day to the crematorium by a different
railroad worker. A monthly subscription cost one 140
gram gold cylinder. Anyone who risked his neck thirty
times a month bringing his newspaper to a KZ prisoner
deserved the sum he received.

Since my arrival in the crematorium I had been the
first one to receive this smuggled copy. I read it in a safe
hiding place, then related the day's events to one of the
prisoner-clerks, who in turn passed on the news to his
companions. Within a few minutes everyone had heard
the latest news.

The Sonderkommando was an elite group; its advantages and privileges have already been noted. In con-
trast to the prisoners in the camp proper, who writhed
in lice-filled boxes, who, mad with hunger, battled furi-
ously for a scrap of bread or a piece of potato, its lot
was indeed good. Fully aware of this unbalanced situation, the Sonderkommando distributed food and clothing to their less fortunate comrades whenever they could.

For the past several days a woman's kommando of
about 500 road workers had been busy not far from the
crematorium gate. They were guarded by two SS and
four police dogs. Their job consisted of carrying rocks
to be used in the construction of a road. Several men
from the Sonderkommando, with the permission of their
own guards, approached the two SS guarding the women
and slipped them each a pack of cigarettes. With that the
deal was concluded. Then three or four women, loaded
with stones, walked over to our gate, as if their work
had brought them there, and immediately gathered up
all the clothing that had been prepared for them. They
also got some bread, bacon and cigarettes. In turn, they
were replaced by others in the kommando, till each had
received her share. There was never any favoritism
shown by the Sonderkommando, for none of us knew

any of the women personally. Overjoyed with their "presents," they returned to their work. The next day a different group replaced them and the same scene was re-enacted.

The crematoriums' enormous storeroom contained great quantities of clothes and shoes awaiting shipment, and I would estimate that several thousand women prisoners were aided in this manner by the Sonderkommando. I also tried to do my bit: loading my pockets with vitamin pills, sulfa tablets, bottles of iodine, bandages and anything else I thought might be useful, I handed them out as the women passed. When my stock was depleted, I returned to my room and refilled my pockets; for those who received them, these medicines often meant the difference between life and death. At least for a little while.

After finishing in number two, I visited number three and number four crematoriums. In number three, besides the Greek and Polish members who made up the majority of the kommando, I noticed that there were already about a hundred Hungarian deportees. In number four the kommando consisted largely of Poles and Frenchmen.

In all these death factories work was in full swing. From the Jewish unloading platform, which was divided into four large finger-like propections, similar to the delta of some flooded river, the victims spilled to their death with maniacal fury. Horrified, I noted with what order and robot-like precision the murders were perpetrated, as if these factories were here for all eternity.

If by chance I ever get out of this place alive, I thought, and have a chance to relate all I've seen and lived through, who will believe me? Words, descriptions are quite incapable of furnishing anyone with an accurate picture of what goes on here. So my efforts to photograph in my mind all I see and engrave it in my memory are, after all, completely useless.

With this discouraging thought running through my mind, I completed my first day's tour of the four crematoriums.

12 I HAD MANAGED TO LAY MY HANDS ON A copy of the French dictionary, *Petit Larousse*. With the help of the maps it contained I tried to situate the names of the various localities mentioned in the newspaper reports. Alone in my room, I studied the military situation along the southern and eastern fronts. Heavy footsteps resounded in the hallway. I quickly flipped the pages and looked impatiently towards the door. The crematorium commander came in to inform me that an important commission was arriving at 2:00 P.M. and that I should have the dissecting room ready to receive them.

Before the commission arrived a hearse pulled up, completely closed and draped with black. Inside lay the body of an SS captain. I had it placed on the dissecting table, still dressed, just as it had been delivered to me.

The commission, consisting of high-ranking, impeccably dressed officers, arrived punctually: an SS Medical Corps Colonel, a judge advocate, two Gestapo officers and a court-martial recorder. A few minutes later Dr. Mengele appeared. I offered them seats. They proceeded to hold a short conference, during which the Gestapo officers related in some detail the circumstances of their colleague's death.

His wounds, caused by a firearm, pointed to either murder or assassination. Suicide was ruled out: the captain's revolver had still been in his holster at the time his body had been discovered. As for the hypothesis that he had been murdered, the crime, they believed, might well have been committed by a fellow officer, or perhaps some subordinate who had had a grievance against him. But assassination seemed even more likely: it was a fairly common occurrence in the Polish city of Gleiwitz and the surrounding area, where groups of partisans were active.

The purpose of the autopsy was to determine whether the shot had been fired from in front or behind, what the caliber and characteristics of the murder weapon were, and from what approximate distance the crime had been committed. At that time there was no doctor at Gleiwitz qualified as a coroner; that was why the body had been brought to Auschwitz for an autopsy, for Gleiwitz was only 40 kilometers away, and Auschwitz was consequently the nearest spot where an autopsy could be performed under satisfactory conditions.

In my role of observer, I stood at a respectful distance from the group while this discussion was taking place, and waited, with the mute patience expected from all KZ prisoners, for Dr. Mengele's instructions.

I had never thought that I, a Jewish prisoner of the KZ, would be allowed to sully—by my contact—the body of an SS officer. As for my performing the autopsy, I would never even have dreamed of it, especially since, even when I had been a so-called "free citizen," racial laws had invariably kept me from giving medical attention to Christians, or, more exactly, to Aryans. So I was quite surprised when Dr. Mengele turned to me and asked me to get on with the dissection.

The first job, far from a simple one, was to undress the body. Two men would be needed to remove his boots alone. I therefore requested permission to call in a couple of assistants. While the body was being undressed, the members of the commission became involved in a heated discussion and paid hardly any attention to me and my helpers.

As I made the initial incision I found myself fighting off an attack of stage fright and a feeling of inferiority. I cut the skin of the skull and, with a quick, precise movement, turned half the skin down over the face and the other half over the back of the neck. The following step was more difficult: it consisted of sawing the skull and removing the brainpan. Almost mechanically I followed, in due order, the prescribed steps.

It was now time to examine the two wounds caused by the bullet. If it had gone all the way through the body there would of course be two holes, one at the point of entrance, the other at the point of exit. In the majority of cases the physician has no trouble telling which is which: the place where the bullet enters the body is always smaller than the point where it emerges. But in the present case there were two holes, exactly the same size, one below the left nipple and the other close to the upper edge of the shoulder blade.

The matter was far from clear, and therefore all the more interesting. What could have caused the uniformity of the two wounds? Dr. Mengele was of the opinion that there might well have been two bullets fired, one from in front and the other from behind. This could easily have been the case if the officer had fallen after the first shot and been hit by the second while he was lying on the ground. Neither bullet went all the way through the body, thus explaining the two identical wounds. This theory sounded plausible enough, but remained to be verified. To do this I had to study the path of the bullet, or bullets. In doing so, I found that the bullet which entered the body below the left nipple pierced the heart, then grazed the left extremity of the spinal column and continued upward at an angle of 35° till it reached the upper edge of the shoulder blade, a tiny portion of which it had crushed before leaving the body. There could be no doubt about it; only one bullet had been fired, and that from in front of the victim, for the path of the bullet moved upward and from front to back at the aforementioned angle of 35°. The reason the two holes were the same size was that the bullet had grazed the spinal column and chipped off a section of the shoulder blade; considerably slowed by these obstacles, it had left the body after most of its energy had been expended. Besides, it is doubtful that anyone would aim downward at an angle of 35° when shooting. To do so would require the murderer to raise his arm well above his head. So it seemed obvious to me that the bullet had been fired from in front, that the weapon had been pointed upward from the horizontal at the time of firing, that the shot had been made at close quarters and that, in all probability, the killer had been prevented by some intervening obstacle from raising his gun any higher. But this was a matter for the inquest to decide.

I saw that my remarks satisfied the members of the commission, for they announced that in the future all cases requiring an autopsy would be sent here. They found this a very satisfactory arrangement. Thus I became, with this one autopsy, the coroner for the KZ in charge of all matters pertaining to forensic medicine in the Gleiwitz district.

13 EARLY ONE MORNING I RECEIVED A PHONE call ordering me to report immediately to the "pyre" for the purpose of bringing back to number one crematorium all the medicines and eyeglasses that had been collected there. After being sorted and classified they would be shipped to various parts of Germany.

The pyre was located about five or six hundred yards from number four crematorium, directly behind the little birch forest of Birkenau, in a clearing surrounded by pines. It lay outside the KZ's electric barbed wire fence, between the first and second lines of guards. Since I was not authorized to venture so far from the actual confines of the camp, I requested some sort of written permission from the office. They issued me a safe conduct good for three persons, for I planned on taking two men with me to help carry the material back to the crematorium.

We set off in the direction of the thick twisting spiral of smoke. All those unfortunate enough to be brought here saw this column of smoke, which was visible from any point in the KZ, from the moment they first descended from the box cars and lined up for selection. It was visible at every hour of the day and night. By day it covered the sky above Birkenau with a thick cloud; by night it lighted the area with a hellish glow.

Our path took us past the crematoriums. After showing the SS guards our safe conduct, we passed through an opening cut in the barbed wire and reached an open road. The surrounding countryside—a patchwork of bright green, grassy clearing—seemed peaceful. But soon my watchful eyes discerned, about a hundred yards away, the guards of the second line, either lounging on the grass or sitting beside their machine guns and police dogs.

We crossed a clearing and came to a small pine forest. Once again we found our way blocked by a fence and gate strung with barbed wire. A large sign, similar to those on the crematorium gates, was posted here:

ENTRANCE IS STRICTLY FORBIDDEN TO ALL THOSE WHO HAVE NO BUSINESS HERE, INCLUDING SS PERSONEL NOT ASSIGNED TO THIS COMMAND.

In spite of this sign, we entered without the guards even asking us for our pass. The reason was simple: the SS guards on duty here were from the crematoriums, and the 60 Sonderkommando men who worked at the pyre were also crematorium personnel from number two. At present the day shift was on. They worked from seven in the morning till seven in the evening, when they were replaced by the night watch, which also consisted of 60 men, taken from number four.

Passing through the gate, we reached an open place which resembled a courtyard, in the middle of which stood a thatched-roof house whose plaster was peeling off. Its style was that of a typical German country house, and its small windows were covered with planks. As a matter of fact, it no doubt had been a country house for at least 150 years, to judge by its thatched roof, which had long since turned black, and its often replastered, flaking walls.

The German State had expropriated the entire village of Birkenau near Auschwitz, in order to establish the KZ there. All the houses, with the exception of this one, had been demolished, and the population evacuated.

What, in fact, must this house have been used for? Had it been meant to be lived in? In that case partitions must have divided the interior into rooms. Or had it originally been one large room, without partitions, meant to be used as a hangar or storeroom? I asked myself these questions, but was unable to supply the answers. In any case, it was now used as an undressing room for those on their way to the pyre. It was here that they deposited their shabby clothes, their glasses, and their shoes.

It was here that the "surplus" from the "Jewish ramp" was sent, that is, those for whom there was no room in the four crematoriums. The worst kind of death awaited them. Here there were no faucets to slake the thirst of several days' voyage, no fallacious signs to allay their misgivings, no gas chamber which they could pretend was a disinfecting room. Merely a peasant house, once painted yellow and covered with thatch, whose windows had been replaced by planks.

Behind the house enormous columns of smoke rose skyward, diffusing the odor of broiled flesh and burning hair. In the courtyard a terrified crowd of about 5,000 souls; on all sides thick cordons of SS, holding leashed police dogs. The prisoners were led, three or four hundred at a time, into the undressing room. There, hustled by a rain of truncheon blows, they spread out their clothes and left the door at the opposite side of the house, yielding their places to those who were to follow. Once out the door, they had no time even to glance around them or to realize the horror of their situation. A Sonderkommando immediately seized their arms and steered them between the double row of SS who lined the twisting path, which, flanked on either side by woods, ran for 50 yards to the pyre, which till now had been hidden by the trees.

The pyre was a ditch 50 yards long, six yards wide and three yards deep, a welter of burning bodies. SS soldiers, stationed at five-yard intervals along the pathway side of the ditch, awaited their victims. They were holding small caliber arms—six millimeters—used in the KZ for administering a bullet in the back of the neck. At the end of the pathway two Sonderkommando men seized the victims by the arms and dragged them for 15 or 20 yards into position before the SS. Their cries of terror covered the sound of the shots. A shot, then immediately afterwards, even before he was dead, the victim was hurled into the flames. Fifty yards farther on a scene similar in all respects was being enacted. Oberschaarführer Molle was in charge of these butchers. As a doctor, and as an eye-witness, I swear that he was the Third Reich's most abject, diabolic and hardened assassin. Even Dr. Mengele showed from time to time that he was human. During the selections at the unloading ramp, when he noticed a healthy young woman who above all wanted to join her mother in the left-hand column, he snarled at her coarsely, but ordered her to regain the right-hand group. Even the ace shot of the number one crematorium, Oberschaarführer Mussfeld, fired a second shot into anyone whom the first shot had not killed outright. Oberschaarführer Molle wasted no time over such trifles. Here the majority of the men were thrown alive into the flames. Woe to any Sonderkommando by whose action the living chain, which extended from cloakroom to pyre, was broken, with the result that one of the members of the firing squad was forced to wait for a few seconds before receiving his new victim.

Molle was everywhere at once. He made his way tirelessly from one pyre to the next, to the cloakroom and back again. Most of the time the deportees allowed themselves to be led without resistance. So paralyzed were they with fright and terror that they no longer realized what was about to happen to them. The majority of the elderly and the children reacted in this way. There were, however, a goodly number of adolescents among those brought here, who instinctively tried to resist, with a strength born of despair. If Molle happened to witness such a scene, he took his gun from his holster. A shot, a bullet often fired from a distance of 40 to 50 yards, and the struggling person fell dead in the arms of the Sonderkommando who was dragging him towards the pyre. Molle was an ace shot. His bullets often pierced the arms of the Sonderkommando men from one side to the other when he was dissatisfied with their work. In such cases he inevitably aimed for the arms, without otherwise manifesting his dissatisfaction, but also without giving any previous warning.

When the two pyres were operating simultaneously, the output varied from five to six thousand dead a day. Slightly better than the crematoriums, but here death was a thousand times more terrible, for here one died twice, first by a bullet in the back of the neck, then by fire.

After death by gas, by chloroform injections, and a bullet in the back of the neck, I had now made my acquaintance with this fourth "combined" method.

I gathered up the medicines and glasses left behind by the victims. Dazed, my knees still trembling with emotion, I started for home, that is, for number one crematorium, which, to quote Dr. Mengele himself, "was no sanatorium, but a place where one could live in a pretty decent way." After having seen the pyres, I was inclined to agree with him.

Once home, I entered the room, but instead of arranging the medicines and spectacles, I took a sedative and went to bed. Today's dose was 30 centigrams, sufficient, I hoped, to counteract the effects of funeral pyre sickness.

14 THE FOLLOWING MORNING I AWOKE WONdering what revelation the new day would bring. For here each new day had its revelation, one more horrible than anything a normal person could ever have dreamed of.

I learned from the Sonder, who invariably managed to have all the latest information, that the KZ was in strict quarantine. This meant that no one could leave the barracks. SS soldiers and their police dogs were out in full force. Today they were going to liquidate the Czech Camp.

The Czech Camp consisted of about 15,000 deportees brought from the Theresienstadt ghetto. Like the Gypsy Camp, it had a family air about it. The deportees had not been "selected" upon arrival, but sent intact to their quarters. All, no matter what their age or physical condition, had been allowed to keep their clean clothes and live together. Their lot was hard, but not unbearable. Unlike the other sections, they did not work.

Thus they had lived for two years, till the hour for their extermination arrived, as sooner or later it arrived for everybody in the KZ. At Auschwitz it was never a question of whether you would live or die, but merely a question of time, of *when* you would die. No one escaped. The trainloads of Hungarian deportees, or, to use the expression current in the KZ, the "freight," arrived in a steady flow, sometimes two trainloads at a time, and disgorged their passengers. For them the ubiquitous Dr. Mengele dispensed with the customary formality of selection. He stood there like a statue, his arm always pointing in the same direction: to the left. Thus whole trainloads were expedited to the gas chambers and pyres.

The quarantine camp, C Camp, D Camp and the F section were terribly overcrowded, despite the quotas which were filled daily for shipment to more distant camps. In the Czech Camp both the children and aged had been greatly weakened by their two-year ordeal: the children's bodies were mere skin and bones, and the elderly prisoners were so weak they could scarcely walk. Both had to relinquish their places to new arrivals who were still strong enough to work.

During the preceding weeks their situation had steadily worsened. When the first Hungarian convoys had begun arriving their rations had been sharply reduced. Then, a few weeks later, when the stream of new deportees had swelled to flood proportions, the camp authorities had found themselves faced with a serious shortage of food. As usual, their remedy had been both drastic and efficient: they had practically suppressed the Czech Camp rations altogether.

Hunger had reduced the prisoners to raving, moaning maniacs. Within a few days their already weakened organisms had disintegrated entirely. Diarrhea, dysentery and typhus had begun their deadly work. Fifty or sixty deaths a day was normal. Their last days were spent in indescribable suffering, till at last death came and set them free.

The closing of all barracks was ordered early in the morning. Several hundred SS soldiers surrounded the Czech area and ordered the inmates to assemble. Their cries of terror as they were loaded onto the waiting vans were terrible to hear, for after two years in the KZ they no longer had any illusions about what lay in store for them. "Liquidation Day" found some 12,000 prisoners left in the Czech Camp. From among that number 1,500 able-bodied men and women were chosen, along with eight physicians. The rest were sent to number two and number three crematoriums. On the following day the Czech Camp was silent and deserted. I saw a truck loaded with ashes leave the crematorium and head towards the Vistula.

Thus the Auschwitz muster rolls were reduced by more than 12,000 "units," and one more bloody page was added to the Auschwitz archives. That page contained only the following brief inscription: "The Czech section of the Auschwitz concentration camp was liquidated this date due to a prevalence of typhus among the prisoners. Signed: Dr. Mengele, *Hauptsturmführer I Lagerazt.*"

The eight physicians from the Czech Camp who, thanks to Dr. Epstein's intervention, had been spared,

were sent to the F Camp's hospital barracks, either because they were physically and mentally exhausted after
their superhuman efforts in caring for their fellow-
prisoners, or because they were infected with typhus.

On the day following the liquidation of the Czech
Camp I paid an official visit to F Camp. There I met the
eight doctors who had escaped death and had a chance to
talk with them, and in particular with Dr. Heller, whose
name was well known in medical circles. From his lips I
learned the full story of the suffering and death of
Czechoslovakia's Jewish elite. Since then, all eight have
perished. They were true doctors. I hold their memory in
deep esteem.

15 THE C CAMP, WHICH WAS SITUATED NEAR
the Czech Camp, was composed of Hungarian Jewish women, often as many as 60,000
at a time, in spite of the daily shipments to distant camps.
It was in this heavily overpopulated camp that the doctors
one day discovered among the inmates of one of the
barracks the symptoms of scarlet fever. By Dr. Mengele's
order that barracks, as well as those on either side of it, was
quarantined. The quarantine lasted only a short time:
from morning till evening, hardly twelve hours. At dusk
trucks arrived to embark the inmates of these three
barracks to the crematoriums. Such were the efficacious
methods employed by Dr. Mengele to prevent the spread
of contagious diseases.

The Czech Camp and C Camp had already felt the
effects of Dr. Mengele's battle against the outbreak of
epidemics. Fortunately, the doctors assigned to these
barracks quickly sized up Dr. Mengele's method for
stemming contagion. And from then on they were careful not to reveal any cases of infectious diseases to the SS
medical authorities. As often as was possible they went so
far as to conceal the sick person in a corner of the barracks, and cared for him as best they could with the

meager resources at their disposal. They avoided at all costs sending the sick to the hospital, since the SS doctors checked all patients there and the appearance of a contagious disease meant the liquidation both of the barracks where the disease had originated and of the neighboring barracks as well. SS medical language called this method "the intensive battle against the spread of infection." The results of that struggle were always one or two truckloads of ashes. . . .

After such precedents, the bodies of two women were brought to me from the B Camp hospital. Dr. Mengele had sent them to me for autopsy. As usual, I received files at the same time which contained detailed medical information on the deceased. In the column headed "diagnosis" I noticed, respectively, the terms "typhoid fever" and "heart failure." The two mentions were followed by question marks.

I am not one usually given to pause and weigh the pro and con before acting. I decide quickly and act quickly, especially when it is a question of an important decision. The results are not always brilliant. The fact that I had ended up here in the crematoriums was the result of a snap decision.

Once again I made up my mind quickly. I could not send Dr. Mengele, in the report on my autopsy, a diagnosis of typhoid fever. The description of the victim's illness was full of loopholes. The diagnosis was accompanied by a question mark. The doctor was obviously unsure of himself in the matter. The autopsy would determine whether or not his judgment had been correct. That was why the two bodies had been sent to me.

I performed the autopsy. The small intestine in both bodies was in an ulcerous state characteristic of three-week-old typhoid. The spleen was also swollen. Beyond all shadow of a doubt, both cases were victims of typhoid fever.

Dr. Mengele arrived as usual about five o'clock in the afternoon. He was in a good humor. He came over and questioned me, full of curiosity as to the results of my autopsies. The two bodies were lying open on the table. The large and small intestines, as well as the spleens from both bodies, were washed and placed in a container, ready to be examined.

I gave him my diagnosis: inflammation of the small

intestine with extensive ulceration. I expounded for Dr. Mengele's benefit the ulcerated state of the small intestine during the third week of typhoid fever, and compared it to the ulcerations which arise during the inflammation of the same organ. I drew his attention to the fact that the swelling of the spleen often accompanied inflammation of the intestine, and that as a consequence it was not a question of typhoid fever, but a serious inflammation of the small intestine, probably caused by meat poisoning.

Dr. Mengele was a race biologist and not a pathologist. So it was not difficult to convince him that my diagnosis was correct. However, to be mistaken annoyed him. Turning to me he said: "If you want my opinion, doctors who are guilty of such crass errors would be more useful to the KZ as road workers than as physicians. Poor diagnoses like these could cause any number of unnecessary deaths."

He took the affidavits and files, but before putting them in his briefcase, added a note in the margin. "Make the women doctors responsible," I read over his shoulder. I sincerely regretted having so wronged my innocent female colleagues, for their diagnosis was excellent. Perhaps they would now lose their jobs and end up performing heavy labor; if Dr. Mengele carried out his threat, I would have been the cause of it.

According to medical customs as practiced outside the barbed wire I had certainly acted unethically, and was fully conscious of my guilt. I had wronged two or three innocent people. But to what lengths might Dr. Mengele have gone in his fight against epidemics, and what might have been the number of victims, if I had acted differently?

The next day, however, I received comforting news concerning the fate of my colleagues. Dr. Mengele had reprimanded them, but had let it go at that. The women doctors stayed on their jobs. Subsequently many bodies were sent to me, with their medical records, but the diagnosis column was never filled out. I preferred it that way. Dr. Mengele's indignation concerning the supposed error in diagnosis nevertheless continued to prey on my mind for several days. To find so much cynicism mixed with so much evil in a doctor surprised me, even in the KZ. He was no ordinary doctor, but a criminal, or rather, a "criminal doctor."

XVI

16 ONE MORNING DR. MENGELE SENT FOR me to report immediately to the F Camp commander. I was happy enough to go, for it would give me a chance to get away from the depressing atmosphere of the crematoriums for a few hours. I knew that the walk would do me good too, for I had little opportunity to exercise. And after the smell of the dissecting room and crematoriums I looked forward to getting a bit of fresh air. Besides, this visit would give me a chance to converse with my F Camp colleagues, who had welcomed me so warmly when I had first arrived in the KZ. I prepared for the trip by filling my pockets with precious medicines and several packages of cigarettes. I did not want to return empty-handed to my former "home" i.e., to hospital-barracks 12.

I left by the iron gate of the crematorium, where the guards noted my number, then headed in the direction of F Camp, without hurrying, the better to enjoy even this short walk. I passed beside the barbed wire fences of the women's camp, the "FKL," where thousands upon thousands of women prisoners were walking to and fro among the flimsy shacks that passed for barracks. All the women looked alike, and all, with their shaven heads and tattered clothes, were repulsive. I thought of my wife and daughter, of their long curly hair, of their stylish clothes and tasteful manner of dressing, of the long hours they used to spend discussing these all-important, feminine problems. Three months had already passed since our separation on the unloading platform. What had become of them? Were they still alive? Together? Were they still in the women's section of the Auschwitz KZ, or had they perhaps been sent to one of the Third Reich's more distant camps? Three months is a long time. But three months in the KZ was longer still. Nevertheless, I had a feeling they were still at Auschwitz. But where? In this complicated labyrinth of barbed wire, which fence was theirs? Everywhere I looked I saw nothing but a vast network of barbed wire, concrete pillars, and signs forbidding entrance or exit. The KZ was nothing but barbed wire; the whole of Germany was encompassed by barbed wire, itself an enormous KZ.

I reached the F Camp gate. The entrance was guarded by the *Blockführerstube*. A soldier and an SS noncom with the face of a brute were on duty. I proceeded to the guardhouse window, pulled up the sleeve of my suitcoat and, in accordance with prescribed procedure, announced my number: A 8450. As I pulled back my sleeve, the wristwatch Dr. Mengele had given me authorization to wear, since I needed it for my work, became visible. To keep such an object was one of the KZ's most heinous offenses. With the speed and fury of a famished tiger the SS noncom jumped to his feet and came running from the guardhouse.

"Who in the devil do you think you are, wearing a wristwatch!" he shouted in a raucous voice. "And what business do you have coming here to F Camp?"

A three months' stay in the crematoriums was a school that left its mark. Without losing my temper, without even batting an eyelash, I answered him in a quiet voice.

"I am here because Dr. Mengele sent for me," I said. "But if it's impossible for me to get into F Camp, then I'd better return to the crematorium and let Dr. Mengele know by telephone."

The name "Dr. Mengele" worked like magic. Just hearing it uttered was enough to make most people tremble. My noncom grew tame in less time than it takes to tell. In an almost fawning manner he asked me just how long I intended staying inside the camp.

"You see, I have to record the information," he added apologetically. I looked at my watch. It was ten o'clock. "I shall stay until 2:00 P.M.," I said. "By then my business with Dr. Mengele will certainly be finished." To punctuate my sentence I took a package of cigarettes from my pocket and handed him a few. Obviously pleased with the gift, he spoke to me in an almost friendly manner, and even went so far as to intimate that he would be most happy to see me on my next visit.

There was no denying it, the name "Dr. Mengele," the mention of the crematorium, and the ostentatious display of cigarettes had made a strong impression on the

SS slave. Now I was certain of being able to spend at least an hour or two with my former friends. But first to find out why Dr. Mengele had sent for me.

I entered the camp commander's barracks and waited in the outer lobby till the clerk asked me my business. I told him. He pointed to a door at the opposite end of the room. I crossed to it and entered a well-furnished study. The walls were covered with graphs and charts which showed what the population and composition of the camp had been during various periods of its existence. Prominently displayed in an ornate frame I noticed an enormous photo-portrait of Himmler, with his pince-nez set delicately on the bridge of his nose.

Three people were seated in the room: Dr. Mengele; Hauptsturmführer Dr. Thilo, head surgeon of the KZ; and Obersturmführer Dr. Wolff, director of the General Medical Service. Dr. Mengele informed Dr. Wolff, whom I had not previously met, that it was I who performed the autopsies in the crematoriums.

"Most interesting," Dr. Wolff said, stroking his chin. "Dr. Mengele has told me of your work. I am especially interested in pathology, Doctor, and would already have looked in on some of your more delicate cases if lack of time had not prevented me."

I waited for what was to follow.

"At the present time," he continued. "I am engaged in a scientific study of some importance. But to round it out I will need your help. That is why I asked Dr. Mengele to have you come over here today." He paused and then went on: "As you know, diarrhea is extremely common in the camp, and 90% of the cases prove fatal. I know all there is to know about the prognosis and evolution of the disease, for I have made thousands of examinations and kept very accurate notes. But my work is imperfect, for, besides clinical observations, a scientific study requires a pathological report on a sufficient number of dysentery cases to be conclusive."

I began to see the light. Dr. Wolff was also engaged in research. In the midst of the stench and smoke of the crematoriums, he too wished to profit from the hundreds of thousands of human guinea pigs available in the KZ, many of whom had been reduced by dysentery to an unbelievable 60 or 65 pounds. Through the dissection of a large number of bodies he hoped to discover the internal manifestations of dysentery still unknown to medical science.

Dr. Mengele wanted to solve the problem of the multiplication of the race by studying the human material—or rather, the twin material—that he was free to employ as he saw fit, Dr. Wolff was searching for the causes of dysentery. Actually, its causes are not difficult to determine; even the layman knows them. Dysentery is caused by applying the following formula: take any individual—man, woman, or innocent child—snatch him away from his home, stack him with a hundred others in a sealed box car, in which a bucket of water has first been thoughtfully placed, then pack them off, after they have spent six preliminary weeks in a ghetto, to Auschwitz. There pile them by the thousands into barracks unfit to serve as stables. For food, give them a ration of mouldy bread made from wild chestnuts, a sort of margarine of which the basic ingredient is lignite, thirty grams of sausage made from the flesh of mangy horses, the whole not to exceed 700 calories. To wash this ration down, a half liter of soup made from nettles and weeds, containing nothing fatty, no flour, no salt. In four weeks, dysentery will invariably appear. Then, three or four weeks later, the patient will be "cured," for he will die in spite of any belated treatment he may receive from the camp doctors.

According to Dr. Wolff, at least 150 bodies would be needed for the chapter of his study devoted to the pathological aspect of the question. Dr. Mengele interrupted the conversation.

"By performing seven autopsies a day," he said, "you should be able to finish the required number in approximately three weeks."

I did not agree. "I'm sorry, gentlemen," I said, "but if you want the job to be accurate and well done—of which I have no doubt—then I can perform only three autopsies a day." After some discussion we finally agreed on this point and, with a cursory nod, I was dismissed.

I paid a call on my colleagues stationed in barracks-hospital number 12. They were overjoyed to receive the medicines I had brought, and contentedly smoked the cigarettes I handed around. Their faces and words betrayed symptoms of fatigue and discouragement. The Czech Camp's sudden and tragic end had had a strong effect on them. Little by little the hopelessness of their situation was overwhelming them, as it had overwhelmed me, but with this difference: my realization had not come little by little, but all at once—the moment I had stepped across the threshold into the crematorium.

I did my best, however, to encourage them, exhorting them to persevere. I described the military situation to them in some detail, and showed how, day by day, it was evolving more and more favorably for us all. Since I read the paper every day I was able to back up my statements with concrete facts. We parted with a round of warm handshakes. In the KZ, the expression "To take leave of a friend is to die a little" took on an added meaning.

In any event I left them feeling that I could say, without fear of boasting, that I have a strong character, for in my own impossible situation I still managed to encourage others to persevere. . . .

Obersturmführer Wolff's former patients, all dead of dysentery, passed in succession beneath the scalpel. I had already finished the first thirty autopsies and was recording the results of my observations. In each case the mucous of the stomach was inflamed, which resulted in a burning, or rather a complete withering of the glands that secrete chloric acid in the stomach. A lack of gastric juices renders digestion impossible, but increases fermentation proportionally.

My second observation concerned the inflamed condition of the small intestine, which was accompanied by a thinning of the intestinal walls. My third observation related to the most important digestive juice of the small intestine, the bile, which is indispensable to the proper assimilation of fats. Opening the liver, I found, instead of a greenish-yellow secretion, an almost colorless liquid which scarcely affected the material still in the intestine and which, in any case, was quite incapable of performing its digestive function.

My fourth observation had to do with the inflammation of the large intestine, which had resulted in a withering, a thinning and an excessive fragility of the intestinal walls, which were about as thick and as strong as cigarette paper. In fact, they were no longer digestive tubes but sewers, through which everything flowed, from one end to the other, in the space of a few minutes.

Such, in outline form, and reduced to a language any layman can understand, are the principal conclusions of my autopsies. The job I had been assigned was in reality monotonous, devoid of any interest whatever. The bacteriological tests were probably being conducted in the village of Risgau, situated about three kilometers from the crematoriums, in the "SS Army's Institute of Hygiene and Bacteriology." There, the renowned Professor Mansfeld, who held the chair of Bacteriology at Pecs Medical School, was in charge of the work.

17 I WAS TAKING MY AFTERNOON NAP WHEN Oberschaarführer Mussfeld, pushing three prisoners ahead of him, entered my room. He informed me that Dr. Mengele had given me three assistants, and so saying he darted a glance in their direction, his expression a mixture of cynicism and pity.

They were indeed pitiful to behold, standing there in dirty rags, dumb from the ill-treatment to which they had been subjected, mortally afraid, and feeling both clumsy and embarrassed by their change of environment. They too had left all hope behind them when they had passed through the crematorium gate.

I extended them a friendly and compassionate hand. We introduced ourselves. The first who took my hand was Dr. Denis Gorog, a physician and pathologist from the state hospital at Szombathely. He was a small, lean man of about 45, who wore thick glasses. He made a favorable impression on me, and I had a feeling we would become good friends. The second was a man of about 50; small, stooped almost to the point of being hunch-backed. He was pot-bellied and had a most disagreeable face. His name was Adolph Fischer. For twenty years he had been the lab assistant at the Prague Pathological Institute. A Czechoslovakian Jew, he had been a KZ prisoner for five years. The third newcomer, Dr. Joseph Kolner, was from Nice, France, and had been interned in the KZ for three years. He was a young man of only 32, not at all loquacious, but most gifted.

Dr. Mengele had fished them out of the D Camp barracks and sent them to me so that the ever-increasing numbers of autopsies could be effected without risk of a bottleneck. I was still responsible for the research undertaken, for the keeping of files and the writing of all reports made on the autopsies performed. The two doctors were going to help me with the dissections, and the lab assistant, faithful to his profession, would prepare the bodies. He would open the skulls, and extract and prepare certain organs for examination. After the dissections he would remove the bodies from the table and see that the dissection room and work room were kept neat and clean.

So I had been given competent, qualified collaborators, who would share my burdens. For me this was an undeniable relief.

18 IN MY ROLE OF SONDERKOMMANDO DOCTOR, I was making my morning rounds. All four crematoriums were working at full blast. Last night they had burned the Greek Jews from the Mediterranean island of Corfu, one of the oldest communities of Europe. The victims were kept for twenty-seven days without food or water, first in launches, then in sealed box cars. When they arrived at Auschwitz's unloading platform, the doors were unlocked, but no one got out and lined up for selection. Half of them were already dead, and the other half in a coma. The entire convoy, without exception, was sent to number two crematorium.

Work was accelerated during the night, so that by morning all that remained of the convoy was a pile of dirty, disheveled clothes in the crematorium courtyard. I gazed sadly at the hill of rags which, little by little, grew wet and soggy beneath a fine autumn rain. Glancing upward, I noticed that the four lightning rods placed at the corners of the crematorium chimneys were twisted and bent, the result of the previous night's high temperatures.

Today, during my rounds a serious case awaited me in number four. One of the Sonderkommando chauffeurs had tried to commit suicide by taking an overdose of sleeping tablets. This was the most common method of committing suicide at Auschwitz. The men of the Sonderkommando had no trouble procuring sleeping tablets, for they found large numbers of them every day when they went through the belongings of the dead.

Approaching his bed, I was moved and chagrined to see that the patient was none other than the "Captain." That was what everyone called him, for no one knew what his real name was. A native of Athens, he had been a captain in the regular army and tutor to the children of the royal family of Greece. He was a polite, intelligent man, with three years of KZ behind him. His wife and children had been sent to the gas chamber as soon as they had arrived. Now, having lost consciousness, he was sleeping peacefully. He had probably taken the sleeping tablets several hours earlier, and yet I found that, for the moment at least, he was in no real danger. The men of the Sonderkommando grouped around his bed asked me softly, and with resignation, "to let the captain go."

"Don't save him," one of them said. "You'll only be prolonging the agony. And you can see for yourself he wanted to escape it now, instead of waiting for the firing squad in a few weeks."

Others offered much the same argument, but I silently went about preparing my instruments. Seeing that their arguments had had no effect, and that I was preparing to inject the antidote, some of the men lost their tempers and spared no words as they told me what they thought of my action. Nevertheless I finished the injections and left the room. Unless he contracted pneumonia during the next five or six days, the Captain would live. Then for several weeks he would continue to stoke the furnaces that burned the bodies of thousands upon thousands of his fellow men, tortured and killed by gas. Till one day the Sonderkommando's final hour would toll, and he and his companions would line up outside the crematorium. A machine-gun blast and all would be over. He and the others would fall, their eyes filled with horror and astonishment.

Now that I was no longer beside his bed, now that his face no longer called forth the doctor in me, the purely human side of my nature was forced to admit that the Captain's friends had been right. I should have "let him go his way," not in front of the cold steel barrel of a machine gun, but in the pleasant narcosis that now enveloped him, where he was free from all moral and physical pain.

I finished my rounds and returned to number one. I glanced around the dissection room and saw that my new colleagues were busy working, with the zeal of neophytes, on the dysentery-racked bodies provided by Dr. Wolff. They were clean shaven and were wearing spotless smocks, new clothes and decent shoes. They looked human again. To see them standing around the dissection table in their white smocks and rubber gloves, anyone unacquainted with the work that went on here might easily have taken this to be the laboratory and dissecting room of some serious scientific institute. But I who had worked here for three months knew that it was not an institute of science, but of pseudo-science. Like the ethnological studies, like the notions of a Master Race, Dr. Mengele's research into the origins of dual births was nothing more than a pseudo-science. Just as false was the theory concerning the degeneracy of the dwarfs and cripples sent to the butchers, in order to demonstrate the inferiority of the Jewish race. To be sure, all this was not to be propagated immediately, for the German people were not yet ready to swallow it. But when the race of Supermen had achieved final victory, having won the war and acquired the territory vital to its needs, then the skeletons of these cripples and dwarfs who had been murdered here would be put on display in the spacious halls of great museums, along with a descriptive plaque giving their name, age, nationality, occupation, etc. Then, on the anniversary of Victory Day, thousands of students of this Third Reich, built to endure a thousand years, would be led through these halls by their professors, to pay homage to their illustrious forebears. Their forebears who, by this victory, and the realization of the sacred mission which History had entrusted to the Master Race, had pushed the surrounding peoples—French, Belgians, Russians, Poles—into the niches corresponding to their inferiority. Better still, they would have completely annihilated one European people, the Jews, who had a long history behind them, a history of 6,000 years, but who had no right to exist a few centuries longer. Why? Because in the course of its long history the Jewish race had degenerated into a people of dwarfs and cripples. By mixing with other races, they had sullied, and threatened to contaminate with degeneracy, the only pure race: the Aryan.

Because of their blood, the Jews were harmful to that great race. Moreover, they were dangerous because their teachers, their artists, their merchants and financiers had become so powerful they threatened to enslave the whole of Europe. By destroying this race the Third Reich's first Führer had given his name immortal stature, and gained the respect and gratitude of all the civilized nations of the world.

It was on the basis of these nonsensical theories that the Nazis waged their war against the rest of the world and destroyed, after deportation, literally all of Europe's Jews, down to the lastborn, suckling babe.

Everything in Germany was false. They called this war a crusade. In their eyes the whole of Russia was a savage steppe, peopled by Mongolian barbarians, themselves a threat to civilization. France was a syphilitic nation, well on its way to dissolution. The English, from their Prime Minister on down, were all incurable alcoholics, suffering for the most part from delirium tremens. While the Japanese, on the other hand, whom most people would be inclined to classify as Mongolians, were considered respectable Aryans, because the exigencies of the moment demanded it.

Their whole outlook on life was a lie. Their daughters and war widows could bear children by any man and receive the thanks of the State for doing so. Children so born could take the name their mother chose for them from among the names of those men, often numerous, to whom she had given herself. The multiplication of the race demanded it. Their cynicism was complete and terrible: details, like the lying signs outside the underground chambers of the crematoriums that announced in seven languages, "BATHS," whereas in reality they were gas chambers; the boxes of cyclon gas,[1] which were labeled,

---

[1] In reply to a query concerning the origin and composition of cyclon gas, Dr. Nyiszli wrote that it was manufactured during the

"POISON: FOR THE DESTRUCTION OF PARASITES," the parasites being, of course, the untold thousands of innocent Jews murdered in the space of a few minutes. Who knows just how far the lie went? Perhaps indeed the signs on the KZ's electric barbed wire also lied; perhaps there was really no 6,000-volt current running through it. But no, that was no lie, for I remember having seen Oberschaarführer Mussfeld's giant wolfhound run into the fence one day, at a point not far from the crematorium gate, and die instantly, electrocuted.

While on the subject of signs, I should not forget to mention the one, read by all prisoners, that was posted at the entrance of the camp. It exhorted them with these words: "FREEDOM THROUGH WORK." Here is a concrete example of what those words really meant. One day a line of box cars stopped at the Auschwitz unloading platform. The doors slid open and 300 prisoners climbed down. Their skin was a lemon yellow color, and they were emaciated beyond all description. When they entered the crematorium courtyard I had a chance to converse with some of them. This is the essence of what they said:

"Three months ago we were shipped away from Auschwitz to work in a factory that manufactures sulphuric acid. When we left there were 3,000 of us, but many died of various and sundry illnesses. Now only 300 of us are left, and we're all suffering from sulphuric poisoning."

They had been told, before being sent back here, that they would be sent for a cure to a rest camp. Half an hour later I saw their blood-spattered bodies lying in front of the crematorium ovens. "Freedom through work!" "Rest camp!" How diabolic can one get? And that is just one of many examples. To cite another: during the months of June and July thousands of postcards were distributed

---

war by the I. G. Farben Co., and that, although it was classified as *Geheimmittel*, that is, confidential or secret, he was able to ascertain that the name "cyclon" came from the abbreviation of its essential elements: *cy*anide, *chlor*ine and *ni*trogen. During the Nuremberg trials the Farben Co. claimed that it had been manufactured only as a disinfectant. However, as Dr. Nyiszli pointed out in his testimony, there were two types of cyclon in existence, type A and type B. They came in identical containers; only the marking A and B differentiated them. Type A was a disinfectant; type B was used to exterminate millions.—*Tr.*

to the inmates of overcrowded barracks, with instructions that they be sent to friends or acquaintances of the prisoners. It was strictly specified that the cards should in no circumstances be headed either "Auschwitz" or "Birkenau," but "Am Waldsee," which is a resort town located not far from the Swiss border. The cards were duly sent, and numerous replies came back. I saw these replies burned, some 50,000 of them according to reliable reports, on a pyre set up in the middle of the crematorium courtyard. To have distributed them to the addressees was quite out of the question, for the latter had preceded the former, that is, the addressees had been burned before the letters. That is the way the matter had been arranged. The purpose of this little scheme had been to allay the fears of the public at large and put an end to the rumors that were rife concerning camps like Auschwitz.

19 IN NUMBER ONE CREMATORIUM'S GAS CHAMBER 3,000 dead were piled up. The Sonderkommando had already begun to untangle the lattice of flesh. The noise of the elevators and the sound of their clanging doors reached my room. The work moved ahead double-time. The gas chambers had to be cleared, for the arrival of a new convoy had been announced.

The chief of the gas chamber kommando almost tore the hinges off the door to my room as he arrived out of breath, his eyes wide with fear or surprise.

"Doctor," he said, "come quickly. We just found a girl alive at the bottom of the pile of corpses."

I grabbed my instrument case, which was always ready, and dashed to the gas chamber. Against the wall, near the entrance of the immense room, half covered with other bodies, I saw a girl in the throes of a death-rattle, her body seized with convulsions. The gas kommando men around me were in a state of panic. Nothing like this had ever happened in the course of their horrible career.

We removed the still-living body from the corpses pressing against it. I gathered the tiny adolescent body into my arms and carried it back into the room adjoining the gas chamber, where normally the gas kommando men change clothes for work. I laid the body on a bench. A frail young girl, almost a child, she could have been no more than fifteen. I took out my syringe and, taking her arm—she had not yet recovered consciousness and was breathing with difficulty—I administered three intravenous injections. My companions covered her body which was as cold as ice with a heavy overcoat. One ran to the kitchen to fetch some tea and warm broth. Everybody wanted to help, as if she were his own child.

The reaction was swift. The child was seized by a fit of coughing, which brought up a thick globule of phlegm from her lungs. She opened her eyes and looked fixedly at the ceiling. I kept a close watch for every sign of life. Her breathing became deeper and more and more regular. Her pulse became perceptible, the result of the injections. I waited impatiently. The injections had not yet been completely absorbed, but I saw that within a few minutes she was going to regain consciousness: her circulation began to bring color back into her cheeks, and her delicate face became human again.

She looked around her with astonishment, and glanced at us. She still did not realize what was happening to her, and was still incapable of distinguishing the present, of knowing whether she was dreaming or really awake. A veil of mist clouded her consciousness. Perhaps she vaguely remembered a train, a long line of box cars which had brought her here. Then she had lined up for selection and, before she knew what was happening, been swept along by the current of the mass into a large, brilliantly lighted underground room. Everything had happened so quickly. Perhaps she remembered that everyone had had to undress. The impression had been disagreeable, but everybody had yielded resignedly to the order. And so, naked, she had been swept along into another room. Mute anguish had seized them all. The second room had also been lighted by powerful lamps. Completely bewildered, she had let her gaze wander over the mass huddled there, but found none of her family. Pressed close against the wall, she had waited, her heart frozen, for what was going to happen. All of a sudden the lights had gone out, leaving her enveloped in total darkness. Something had stung her eyes, seized her throat, suffocated her. She had fainted. There her memories ceased.

Her movements were becoming more and more animated; she tried to move her hands, her feet, to turn her head left and right. Her face was seized by a fit of convulsions. Suddenly she grasped my coat collar and gripped it convulsively, trying with all her might to raise herself. I laid her back down again several times, but she continued to repeat the same gesture. Little by little, however, she grew calm and remained stretched out, completely exhausted. Large tears shone in her eyes and rolled down her cheeks. She was not crying. I received the first reply to my questions. Not wanting to tire her, I asked only a few. I learned that she was sixteen years old, and that she had come with her parents in a convoy from Transylvania.

The kommando gave her a bowl of hot broth, which she drank voraciously. They kept bringing her all sorts of dishes, but I could not allow them to give her anything. I covered her to her head and told her that she should try and get some sleep.

My thoughts moved at a dizzy pace. I turned towards my companions in the hope of finding a solution. We racked our brains, for we were now face to face with the most difficult problem: what to do with the girl now that she had been restored to life? We knew that she could not remain here for very long.

What could one do with a young girl in the crematorium's Sonderkommando? I knew the past history of the place: no one had ever come out of here alive, either from the convoys or from the Sonderkommando.

Little time remained for reflection. Oberschaarführer Mussfeld arrived to supervise the work, as was his wont. Passing by the open door, he saw us gathered in a group. He came in and asked us what was going on. Even before we told him he had seen the girl stretched out on the bench.

I made a sign for my companions to withdraw. I was going to attempt something I knew without saying was doomed to failure. Three months in the same camp and in the same milieu had created, in spite of everything, a certain intimacy between us. Besides, the Germans generally appreciate capable people, and, as long as they need them, respect them to a certain extent, even in the KZ. Such was the case for cobblers, tailors, joiners and locksmiths. From our numerous contacts, I had been able to ascertain that Mussfeld had a high esteem for the medical expert's professional qualities. He knew that my superior was Dr. Mengele, the KZ's most dreaded figure, who, goaded by racial pride, took himself to be one of the most important representatives of German medical science. He considered the dispatch of hundreds of thousands of Jews to the gas chambers as a patriotic duty. The work carried on in the dissecting room was for the furtherance of German medical science. As Dr. Mengele's pathological expert, I also had a hand in this progress, and therein lay the explanation for a certain form of respect that Mussfeld paid me. He often came to see me in the dissecting room, and we conversed on politics, the military situation and various other subjects. It appeared that his respect also arose from the fact that he considered the dissection of bodies and his bloody job of killing to be allied activities. He was the commandant and ace shot of number one crematorium. Three other SS acted as his lieutenants. Together they carried out the "liquidation" by a bullet in the back of the neck. This type of death was reserved for those who had been chosen in the camp, or else sent from another on their way to a so-called "rest camp." When there were merely 500 or less, they were killed by a bullet in the back of the neck, for the large factory of gas chambers was reserved for the annihilation of more important numbers. As much gas was needed to kill 500 as to kill 3,000. Nor was it worthwhile to call out the Red Cross truck to bring the canisters and gas butchers for such a trifling number of victims. Nor was it worth the trouble of having a truck come to collect the clothes, which were scarcely more than rags anyway. Such were the factors which determined whether a group would die by gas or by a bullet in the back of the neck.

And this was the man I had to deal with, the man I had to talk into allowing a single life to be spared. I calmly related the terrible case we found ourselves confronted with. I described for his benefit what pains the child must have suffered in the undressing room, and the horrible scenes that preceded death in the gas chamber.

When the room had been plunged into darkness, she had breathed in a few lungfuls of cyclon gas. Only a few, though, for her fragile body had given way under the pushing and shoving of the mass as they fought against death. By chance she had fallen with her face against the wet concrete floor. That bit of humidity had kept her from being asphyxiated, for cyclon gas does not react under humid conditions.

These were my arguments, and I asked him to do something for the child. He listened to me attentively, then asked me exactly what I proposed doing. I saw by his expression that I had put him face to face with a practically impossible problem. It was obvious that the child could not remain in the crematorium. One solution would have been to put her in front of the crematorium gate. A kommando of women always worked there. She could have slipped in among them and accompanied them back to the camp barracks after they had finished work. She would never relate what had happened to her. The presence of one new face among so many thousands would never be detected, for no one in the camp knew all the other inmates.

If she had been three or four years older that might have worked. A girl of twenty would have been able to understand clearly the miraculous circumstances of her survival, and have enough foresight not to tell anyone about them. She would wait for better times, like so many other thousands were waiting, to recount what she had lived through. But Mussfeld thought that a young girl of sixteen would in all naïveté tell the first person she met where she had just come from, what she had seen and what she had lived through. The news would spread like wildfire, and we would all be forced to pay for it with our lives.

"There's no way of getting round it," he said, "the child will have to die."

Half an hour later the young girl was led, or rather carried, into the furnace room hallway, and there Mussfeld sent another in his place to do the job. A bullet in the back of the neck.

20 NEXT DOOR TO THE SS LIVING QUARTERS, on the second story of number two crematorium, was a carpenter's shop, where three carpenters plied their trade, fulfilling any and all requests that were sent to them. For the moment they were busy filling a "private order." Oberschaarführer Mussfeld, taking advantage of the opportunity, had ordered the carpenters to make him a "recamier," a sort of double bed that could also serve as a large sofa. It was to be completed as quickly as possible.

It was no easy job, but in the crematoriums there was no such word as "impossible" when an order was given. The carpenters had salvaged the necessary wood from among the construction materials scattered about the crematorium grounds. The springs had come from the easy chairs that certain deportees had brought with them to make the journey more comfortable for their ailing parents. There were hundreds of these abandoned chairs in the crematorium courtyard and we used to sit in them after work to rest awhile and catch a few breaths of fresh air.

So the recamier was built according to instructions. For me it had become an object of curiosity. I had followed all phases of its construction and seen it completed. I had watched them install the springs and cover them with elegant tapestries. Two French electricians had installed a bed lamp and arranged a niche for a radio. After it had been varnished it was quite handsome. In a small bourgeois home in Mannheim it would look even better than it did up in the uninviting crematorium loft. For the recamier was to be sent, at the end of the week, to Mussfeld's home at Mannheim. There it would wait till the victorious *Ober,* back from the trying wars, could use it to rest his weary bones.

One day, the week prior to its shipment. I was in my room and saw a half dozen silk pajamas—a natural sup-

plement for the recamier—waiting to join the package.
They were of fine imported silk and would certainly
have been unobtainable on the outside, where ration
tickets were needed for even the most essential items.
The KZ also had its ration system, a much better one
than that in force throughout Germany, for it furnished those who used it with any item they desired. In
the undressing room the goods were there waiting to be
taken. It only took one point per item, a point of flame
from the *Ober*'s gun, sending a bullet into the back of
the owner's neck.

In exchange for these "points" the SS officials received jewelry, leather goods, fur coats, silks and fine
shoes. Not a week went by without their sending some
packages home.

In the packages that had been sent one found, besides
the luxury items already mentioned, tea, coffee, chocolate, and canned goods by the hundreds, all of which
were also obtainable in the undressing room. Thus the
Ober had conceived the idea of having a recamier constructed and sent home.

As I watched, day by day, the final phases of its construction, an idea began to take shape in my mind. Little
by little the idea transformed itself into a project. In a
few weeks the Sonderkommando would be a thing of
the past. We would all perish here, and we were well
aware of it. We had even grown used to the idea, for
we knew there was no way out. One thing upset me
however. Eleven Sonderkommando squads had already
perished and taken with them the terrible secret of the
crematoriums and their butchers. Even though we did
not survive, it was our bounden duty to make certain that
the world learned of the unimaginable cruelty and sor-
didness of a people who pretended to be superior. It was
imperative that a message addressed to the world leave
this place. Whether it was discovered soon afterwards,
or years later, it would still be a terrible manifesto of ac-
cusation. This message would be signed by all the members of number one crematorium's Sonderkommando,
fully conscious of their impending death. Carried beyond
the barbed wires of KZ in the recamier, it would remain
for the time being at Oberschaarführer Mussfeld's home
at Mannheim.

The message was drafted in time. It described in sufficient detail the horrors perpetrated at Auschwitz from the time of its founding until the present. The names of the camp's torturers were included, as well as our estimate of the number of people exterminated, with a description of the methods and instruments utilized for extermination.

The message was drawn up on three large sheets of parchment. The Sonderkommando's editor, a painter from Paris, copied it in beautifully written letters, as was the custom with ancient manuscripts, using India ink so that the writing would not fade. The fourth sheet contained the signatures of the Sonderkommando's 200 men. The sheets were fastened together with a silk thread, then rolled up, enclosed in a specially constructed cylindrical tube made of zinc by one of our tinsmiths, and finally sealed and soldered so as to protect the manuscript from air and humidity. Our joiners placed the tube in the recamier's springs, among the wool floss of the upholstering.

Another message, exactly the same, was buried in the courtyard of number two crematorium.

21 I HAD BECOME USED TO SEEING A TRUCK enter the crematorium gate every evening about seven o'clock, carrying 70 to 80 men and women on their way to be liquidated. Coming from the barracks hospital, they represented the KZ's daily selection. Prisoners for several years, or at least for several months, they were fully aware of the fate awaiting them. When the truck entered the courtyard the walls resounded with the screams and cries of the damned. They knew that at the foot of the crematory ovens all hope of escape dissolved.

Not wanting to witness that daily scene, I generally withdrew to the most remote corner of the crematorium courtyard, where I sat down under an arbor of pines. The crackling of the revolvers and the screams were deadened by the time they reached me.

One evening, however, my luck ran out. From five o'clock on I was working in the dissecting room. I had to examine the suicide case of an SS Oberschaarführer whose body had been sent me from Gleiwitz. An SS captain—one of the court-martial judges—and a clerk sat in on the dissection.

About seven o'clock, while I was dictating the affidavit to the SS clerk, the heavy truck loaded with prisoners entered the courtyard. Two windows, barred and covered with metal mosquito netting, looked out on the crematorium's rear courtyard. All the occupants were extremely calm. From this I deduced that they had been selected not out of the barracks, but from the hospitals. They were all seriously ill, too weak to scream or even to climb down from the raised platform of the truck.

The SS guards became excited and began to shout, urging them to get down. No one moved. The driver also began to lose patience. He climbed back in the truck and started the motor. Little by little the truck's immense dump began to rise, till suddenly it spilled the occupants to the ground, a writhing, slipping, frantically grasping mass. As they fell they bumped against each other striking their heads, their faces, their knees against the concrete. Then at last a horrible, collective cry of pain burst forth and echoed throughout the courtyard.

The SS court-martial judge, drawn by the moans and shouts, interrupted his investigations to ask me: "What's going on in the courtyard?" He came over to the window, where I explained to him just what was happening. Apparently he was not used to such scenes, for he turned his head away and said disapprovingly, "Nevertheless, they shouldn't do that!"

The Sonderkommando stripped them of their clothes and piled the discarded rags in the courtyard. The victims were led into the incineration rooms and put in front of the Oberschaarführer's revolver barrel. Mussfeld was today's killer on duty. Standing near the ovens, wearing rubber gloves, he held his weapon with a steady hand. One by one the bodies fell, each yielding his place to the next in line. Within a few minutes he had "tumbled"—that was the term in general usage—the eighty men. Half an hour later they had all been cremated.

Later Mussfeld paid me a visit and asked me to give

him a physical check up. He suffered from heart trouble and severe headaches. I checked his blood pressure, took his pulse, listened to his heart with a stethoscope. His pulse rate was slightly high. I gave him my opinion: his condition was no doubt the result of the little job he had just performed in the furnace room. I had wanted to reassure him, but the result was just the opposite. He became indignant, got up and said:

"Your diagnosis is incorrect. It doesn't bother me any more to kill 100 men than it does to kill 5. If I'm upset, it's merely because I drink too much."

And so saying he turned and walked away, greatly displeased.

22 I WAS IN THE HABIT OF READING FOR awhile in bed each night before I went to sleep. One night, while I was doing just that, the lights suddenly went out and the KZ alarm siren began its dismal wail. Whenever there was an alert we were taken, convoyed by well-armed SS guards, to the Sonderkommando shelter, that is, to the gas chamber.

We crossed the threshold of the gas chamber with heavy hearts. The whole kommando was present, 200 strong. It was a terrible feeling to remain in this room, knowing that hundreds of thousands of people had met a frightful end here. Besides, we knew that the life of the Sonderkommando was drawing to a close. This being the case, the SS could very easily have closed the gas chamber doors and dumped four cases of cyclon gas down the chimneys to liquidate us all.

As a matter of fact, such action would not have been without precedent. A part of the eleventh Sonderkommando had been transferred from the D quarter to Barracks 13, a restricted area, and informed that, upon orders from above, the group would no longer live in the crematoriums, but henceforth in this barracks. They would continue to work at the oven, however, going in two separate groups from the barracks to the crematorium. That same evening they had been taken to the D quarter for a bath and a change of clothing. After the bath they had been pushed into a neighboring room to get disinfected clothes. This room was a real disinfecting chamber, and as such could be hermetically sealed. Normally, that was where the lice-filled clothes collected in the camp were disinfected. Four hundred men from the Sonderkommando were liquidated in this manner. From there, trucks took their bodies to the funeral pyre.

Thus our anxiety while waiting for the alert to be over was not unfounded. This one lasted for three hours. Then we came up out of darkness to see the long kilometers of barbed wire once again lighted by the searchlights, and returned to bed. I tried to fall asleep, but sleep was slow in coming.

The following day, while making my rounds in number two crematorium, the chief of the Sonderkommando there informed me confidentially that during the alert the previous night a group of partisans had slipped into the camp. In an out-of-the-way spot they had cut the barbed wire surrounding the courtyard and slipped three machine guns and twenty hand grenades through the opening. The Sonderkommando men had discovered them early that morning and hidden them in a safe place.

This news gave us some slight hope for the future. We knew that the hands that had smuggled us these weapons could not be far off. From a series of observations I was inclined to believe that the local underground was operating about 25 to 30 kilometers from the camp. We hoped that, under cover of the next alert, they would manage to slip us some more weapons. Recently there had been alerts every day. But for us the only ones that really counted were those that occurred at night and lasted a relatively long time, for only then could our anonymous and devoted friends get close to the camp. After three or four alerts, we would perhaps have enough arms to try and force our way past the guards.

The organization for this future operation was coordinated by number three crematorium, and had contacts in all the others. The whole affair was being conducted with the utmost care and circumspection. Death stalked our every move, in the form of the lethal machine guns manned by our guards. We wanted to live. We wanted to get out of here. But even if most of us failed to make it, even if only one or two escaped, we would still have won out, for there would then be someone to tell the world about the dark mysteries of these death factories.

As for those destined to pay with their lives, at least they would not have died like worms, crushed by their butchers' unclean hands. On the contrary, they would be the first in the history of the KZ who, despite overwhelming odds in both numbers and material, would have sowed death and destruction among their torturers before dying proudly like men.

23 ANNIHILATION TIME HAD COME FOR THE 4,500 inhabitants of the Gypsy Camp. The measures taken were the same as those taken for the liquidation of the Czech Camp. All the barracks were quarantined. SS guards, leading their police dogs, invaded the Gypsy quarters and chased the inhabitants outside, where they were made to line up. Rations of bread and salami were distributed. The gypsies were made to believe that they were being shipped to another camp, and they swallowed the story. A very easy and efficacious way of calming their fears. No one thought of the crematoriums, for then why would rations of food have been distributed?

This strategy on the part of the SS was dictated neither by pity nor a regard for those condemned to death, but merely by their desire to expedite a large group of people, without any unnecessary incidents or delays, to the gas chambers, guarded by a relatively small patrol. The strategy worked to perfection. Everything went off as planned. Throughout the night the chimneys of numbers one and two crematoriums sent flames roaring skyward, so that the entire camp was lighted with a sinister glow.

Next day the Gypsy Camp, once so noisy, lay silent

and deserted. The only sound was the monotonous chant of the barbed wires rubbing together, while the doors and windows left open banged and squeaked endlessly under the powerful wind of the Volhynian steppes.

Once again Europe's pyromaniacs had organized a gigantic display of fireworks. Once again the setting was the Auschwitz concentration camp. This time, however, the victims thrown to the flames were not Jews, but Christians: Catholic gypsies from Germany and Austria. By morning their bodies had been transformed into a pile of silvery ashes rising in the crematorium courtyard. The bodies of twelve sets of twins had not been consigned to the flames. Even before sending them to the gas chamber, Dr. Mengele had marked a Z.S. on their chests with his special chalk.

In this collection of bodies there were twins of all ages, ranging from newborn infants to sixteen-year-olds. For the moment, the twelve pairs of corpses were stretched out on the concrete floor of the "morgue." Bodies of black-haired, dark-skinned children. The job of classifying them by pairs was a tiring one. I was careful not to mix them up, for I knew that if I should render these rare and precious speciments unusable for his research, Dr. Mengele would make me pay for it with my life.

Only a few days before I had been sitting with him in the work room, near the table, looking through the records already set up on twins, when he noticed a faint spot of grease on the bright blue cover of one of the files. I often handled the records in the course of my dissections, and had probably spotted it with a bit of grease. Dr. Mengele shot a withering glance at me and said, very seriously:

"How can you be so careless with these files, which I have compiled with so much love!"

The word "love" had just crossed Dr. Mengele's lips. I was so taken aback that I sat there dumbfounded, unable to think of anything to say in reply.

24 I CONDUCTED THE PATHOLOGICAL STUDY OF the twelve pairs of twins with the greatest possible care. As everyone knows, there are two kinds of twins, one-egg and two-egg. Twins born of the same egg are always identical, both in their internal and external manifestation, and of the same sex. They are variously known as identical, uniovular or monozygotic. Twins born from two separate eggs resemble one another in both their internal and external characteristics, but rather as brothers and sisters do. They are not perfectly identical and, in about half the cases, are of different sexes. They are known as fraternal, biovular or dizygotic.

These remarks constitute, medically speaking, one of the basic laws of heredity concerning twins. This law has been used extensively by those who claim that environmental factors, such as education, nutrition, the illnesses a person may have suffered, etc., influence only slightly his physical, mental and temperamental makeup, whereas heredity plays a much more important role. If the traits a person has received from his forebears occur again and again throughout several generations, they are known as dominant hereditary characteristics.

These dominant hereditary characteristics can either be to the advantage or disadvantage of the individual. For example, a good healthy set of teeth, a thick head of hair that does not thin with the years, or hypertension and, in some families, diabetes. Among the mental illnesses, nervous depression.

These hereditary phenomena, whether they are advantageous or disadvantageous, often appear at birth: a child born with too many fingers or toes would be an example. Other phenomena develop later on and become chronic illnesses, such as epilepsy, asthma, gout, certain forms of hypertension, a few cases of cancer, and the senile cataract of the ocular lens, this last occurring only in people sixty or older.

101

Among these hereditary phenomena one sometimes finds this peculiarity, that they occur more often in one sex than in the other. Daltonism, or congenital color-blindness, and anemia are two of the most frequent manifestations of these hereditary phenomena defined by sex. Both of these illnesses appear only in males, never in females. Anemia is the most obvious example: the most common hereditary form of anemia is that which has passed from an anemic grandfather through a healthy daughter to half the male grandchildren. Male children never inherit it directly from an anemic father. Each male child and all of his descendents will remain healthy, whether they be male or female. But the female children of an anemic father will, though in themselves healthy, carry the seeds of anemia, and each of their daughters will transmit the seeds to their male offspring.

I had the bodies of a pair of fifteen-year-old twins before me on the dissection table. I began a parallel and comparative dissection of the two bodies. Nothing particularly noteworthy about the heads. The next phase was the removal of the sternum. Here an extremely interesting phenomenon appeared: a persistent thymus, that is, a thymus gland that continued to subsist. Normally the thymus is found only in children. It extends from the upper edge of the sternum to the heart, thus covering a fairly large area. With puberty it begins to wither rapidly and soon disappears completely. Once sexual maturity has been attained, all that is left of it is a small pocket of fat, plus the remains of the fibrous tissues of the former gland.

The thymus has a great influence on growth. When it withers too rapidly, the individual will be small, perhaps even a dwarf, and besides, his tibular bones will be very fragile. Overdevelopment, or hypersecretion of the gland, is often found during the autopsy of children who have died suddenly for no apparent reason, without having been ill. Hypersecretion is also frequently found in young people who prove to be excessively vulnerable to infectious diseases.

Thus the discovery of the thymus gland in the twin brothers was of considerable interest, for not only was it still extant here in these fifteen-year-olds, whereas it should have disappeared at the age of twelve, but it was, besides, abnormally large. I dissected two other sets of twins, one of fifteen years of age and the other of sixteen, and found the thymus withered in both cases.

From each of the eight identical twins I extracted the cervical part of the spinal column. The fourth and fifth vertebrae presented an anomaly: these vertebrae had not closed up at the age of twelve or thirteen, but remained open, even in the case of the fifteen- and sixteen-year-old twins. This anomaly, called "spina bifide," is a pathological state whose consequences can be extremely serious.

An individual develops in both directions of the spinal column, that is, upward towards the cranium and downward towards the pelvis, or rather, the caudal bone. Development is called cranial or caudal, depending on the predominant tendency. In the present case the tendency was cranial for all the twins, since the "spina bifide" and the transverse bone which had remained open were degenerate phenomna.

Another anomaly I found in the five pairs of twins was the non-fixation of the tenth rib. Normally, this rib is attached to the sternum. The fact that it was "floating" resulted from an irregularity of the spinal column's growth in the pelvic direction.

I committed these curious observations to paper, in a much more precise and scientific manner than I have employed to describe them here, for my dissection report. Later I spent a long afternoon in deep discussion with Dr. Mengele, trying to clear up a certain number of doubtful points. In the dissection room and laboratory I was no longer a humble KZ prisoner, and I consequently defended and explained my point of view as though this were a medical conference of which I were a full-fledged member. I contradicted Dr. Mengele on several occasions, and completely disagreed with one of his hypotheses.

I know men, and it seemed to me that my firm attitude, my measured sentences, and even my silences were the qualities by which I had succeeded in making Dr. Mengele, before whom the SS themselves trembled, offer me a cigarette in the course of a particularly animated discussion, proving he forgot for a moment the circumstances of our relationship.

25 ONCE WHEN I WAS DISSECTING THE BODY of a fairly old man, I discovered some very beautiful gallstones in the bladder. Knowing that Dr. Mengele was an ardent collector of such items, I washed the stones, dried them, and then arranged them in a large-necked flask, stoppered with a glass cork. I stuck a label on the flask, giving the person's name, the kind of stones they were, and their pathological characteristics. During his visit next day, I gave them to Dr. Mengele. He admired the beautiful crystals. Turning the flask round and round, he looked at the gallstones and then, turning abruptly to me, asked if I knew the ballad of the warrior Wallenstein. His question was completely out of keeping with the surroundings, but I answered: "I know the story of the warrior Wallenstein, but not the ballad." Whereupon, smiling, he began to recite:

*"Im Besitze der Familie Wallenstein
Ist mehr Gallenstein, wie Edelstein."*

which, translated into English, would go something like:

*"In the Wallenstein family
There are more gallstones than precious stones."*

My superior recited several stanzas of that comic ballad. He was in such a good mood that I decided to ask a great favor of him: that he let me go look for my wife and child. Only after I had uttered the request did I realize how daring it was: but it was already too late. He looked at me with astonishment.

"You're married and have a child?"

"Yes, Captain, I'm married and have a fifteen-year-old daughter," I told him, my voice breaking with emotion.

"Do you think they are still here?" he asked.

"Yes, Captain, because at our arrival three months ago you selected them and sent them to the right-hand column."

"They may have since been sent on to another camp," he said. Suddenly I thought of the crematorium smoke: perhaps they had since been dispatched with that smoke to some celestial camp. Dr. Mengele, who was seated, his head bent forward, seemed lost in thought. I remained standing behind him.

"I'm going to give you a pass to go look for them, but . . ." and placing his forefinger on his lips, he looked at me menacingly.

"I understood, Captain, and thank you."

Dr. Mengele left. I returned to my room, completely elated, holding the pass in my hand. Once there I began to read it: "Number A 8450 is authorized to circulate freely within the confines of the Auschwitz KZ. Signed: Dr. Mengele, SS Hauptsturmführer." Never to my knowledge had anything like this happened in the history of the camp. I did not know quite where to begin. The women were quartered in the C, B3 and FK4 Camps. As far as I knew, most of the Hungarian women were in C Camp. I decided to try there first.

The following day I got up still tired, not having slept a wink all night. Terrible doubts assailed me. Here, where three months was an eternity, so many things could have happened to them. My position in the KZ had made me realize only too well everything that went on inside these bloody walls.

I entered the SS office to announce my departure, and bid my comrades good-bye. They wished me luck. Althought it was still early, the white August sun was already scorching hot when I set out on my three kilometer journey. As the crow flies, C Camp was considerably closer, but I had to keep within the fences, and was therefore obliged to make numerous detours. Filled with a mixture of dread and curiosity, I set out through the neutral zone, which was bordered by electrified fences. They never fired on you without warning when you passd through the maze of wires. Motorcycle patrols rode by with signs hung round their necks reading: "Lagerpolizei": "Camp Police." I met several of them on my way, but none molested me.

Reaching C Camp, I saw an immense iron gate looming before me, whose two wings bore numerous porcelain insulators, reinforced by barbed wire. In front of the gate, the inevitable guard house. Some SS soldiers were basking in the sun. They looked me up and down, for I was an unusual guest, but said nothing. They did not bother about business that concerned only their comrade seated near the guard house window.

I approached the latter and gave him my tattoo number. He looked at me expectantly. I took Dr. Mengele's pass from my pocket and handed it to him. After perusing it, he ordered his comrades to open the gates, then asked me how long I wanted to stay inside, for, as always, he had to record it in his register.

"Until noon," I said evenly. Two hours was a great deal to ask, but the customary bribe of a package of cigarettes was sufficient to get his assent. I handed him a pack and passed through the gate.

The main road of C Camp, bordered by dilapidated, faded green barracks, was animated. A women's detail was carrying a large iron cask filled with hot soup, for here the noon meal was distributed at 10 o'clock. Another group—a highway kommando—was busily engaged carrying stones for repairing the camp roads. Several women were stretched out in the sun along both sides of this main thoroughfare. Their bodies were clothed in rags, their heads were shaven; they were indeed a pitiful sight to behold. Many were dressed in the most fantastic clothing—one was wearing a sleeveless evening gown—and were seated on the ground, busy delousing themselves or their companions. The exposed parts of their bodies were covered with foul, oozing sores. It was from this section that convoys were chosen to be sent to camps farther away. As far as I could tell the selections had been very carefully made, for all those left here appeared to be the very weakest. Lucky were they who had been sent to more distant camps, for they still had a chance of surviving, whereas the fate of those still here was sealed, a fate identical to that of the Gypsy Camp.

I headed towards the first barracks. From all sides cries and shouts greeted me. Those who had seemingly been mere bundles of rags lying on the ground or crawling on all fours revived and, leaving their places, ran towards me. About thirty of them had recognized me and crowded around asking anxiously for news of their husbands and children.

If they had been able to récognize me it was because I had managed to live in such a way that I still looked like a human being. But it was almost impossible for me to recognize them, so greatly had they changed. My situation in the middle of the clamoring crowd was becoming embarrassing. In ever-increasing numbers they crowded around me. Everyone wanted to learn something about her family. For three months they had been living under an impossible regime and in constant fear. Here selection took place once a week. Three months had been long enough for them to have learned to regret the past and fear the future.

The women asked me if everything they had heard about the crematoriums was true. What was the smoke you saw pouring from the chimneys during the day, and the flames that replaced it at night? I tried to reassure them, denying everything.

"It's not true," I repeated after each of their questions and surmises. "Besides, the war is almost over and soon we'll all be back home." I said it without really believing it myself.

I left them without having learned any news of my wife and daughter. I entered the first barracks and asked the overseer, a young Slovakian girl, to have the names of my wife and daughter called out. There were between 800 and 1,000 women stacked one above the other on the berths that lined the walls of every barracks. To have the names called out here was not easy. The noise of the thousand women drowned the single voice. The overseer returned a few minutes later to tell me that her search had proved fruitless. I thanked her for her kindness and entered the second barracks.

Here the situation was much the same; the same scene was repeated with like results. I was in the third barracks, standing in the middle of the room. Again I had the overseer called and asked her to have my wife and daughter sent for. She sent two little girls down each side of the barracks; they stopped at each layer of bunks and called out the names. In a few minutes they returned bringing my wife and daughter with them!

They approached hand in hand, their eyes wide with fear, knowing the probable consequences of a personal summons. But they had already recognized me. They stopped dead; astonished, rooted to the spot. I approached them, took both of them in my arms, and embraced them. They were incapable of speaking, but were satisfied to cry softly. I tried to console them, to reassure them, but already the crowd surrounded us. Under such conditions there was absolutely no way of holding a conversation. I asked the overseer if she would let us have the use of her little room for a few minutes. Then, at last, we were alone.

They brought me up to date on their sad experiences of the previous three months: the dreaded selections, from which they had till now escaped, but the very thought of which made them tremble with fear, living as they did in the shadow of the crematorium chimneys. Dressed in rags, they suffered from cold and perpetual hunger. It rained in their barracks and their clothes never dried out completely. The food was uneatable and, what was worse, they were unable to sleep. The place assigned to them was meant to hold seven people; twelve were stacked in there. Women whose social rank back home was fairly high pushed and shoved each other in order to give themselves a few inches more space, thus hoping to sleep a little better, even if it was at the expense of their companions. Everybody here had lost her former personality. Friends or strangers, each was concerned only about her own well-being, unwilling to make the slightest concession. My daughter told me that she slept on the concrete floor, since nobody would make a place for her on the bunk where her mother slept. My wife asked me about my work. I explained to her that I was Dr. Mengele's assistant, and as such a member of the Sonderkommando. After three months of KZ life they too had learned that the Sonder was the kommando of the living dead. Both looked at me aghast. I reassured them as best I could and promised to return the following day.

The fact that I had found my wife and child made sensational news at the crematorium. I took warm clothing, linen and stockings from the clothing department, toothbrushes, nail cutters, penknives and combs from the toilet article section. From the pharmacy I got a stock of vitamin pills, ointment for their sores, and anything else I thought might be useful. I got a sizable quantity, much more than was necessary for my wife and daughter. Besides, I filled my sack with blocks of sugar, butter, jam and bread in quantities large enough to be able to distribute them to the other prisoners. So it was that I left for the C Camp with my sack bulging. But all good things must come to an end.

For three weeks I visited C Camp every day. One day what I was afraid would happen actually came to pass. I had already come to the conclusion, after the liquidation of the Czech and Gypsy Camps, that extermination was merely a matter of chronological order. Sooner or later the time came for all those who spent their days of misery within the confines of Auschwitz's barbed wire barriers.

One afternoon I was seated at my work table in the laboratory. Dr. Mengele and Dr. Thilo were present, discussing questions pertaining to the KZ's administration. Dr. Mengele, as though he had just reached a decision, got up from his chair and said to Dr. Thilo: "I am no longer able to feed the debilitated prisoners of C Camp. I shall have them liquidated during the next two weeks."

Such scenes often took place in my presence. Affairs of a most confidential nature were discussed as though I were not even there. Was I not after all a living dead man, whose presence no longer meant anything?

I was deeply shaken by Dr. Mengele's decision concerning the liquidation of C Camp, for it concerned not only my immediate family, but thousands of my unfortunate compatriots. I had to act immediately.

As soon as Dr. Mengele and Dr. Thilo left the crematorium, I followed them and headed directly for D Camp, where the SS group which supervised the incorporation of foreign prisoners into forced labor battalions was installed. In this camp the prisoners necessary for that program of slave labor in force throughout all Germany were portioned out. The head was an Oberschaarführer. I found him alone in his room. I introduced myself and showed him Dr. Mengele's pass.

I explained to him that my wife and child were interned in C Camp. After having tracked them down with Dr. Mengele's help, I had been doing all I could for them. Nevertheless, I knew the fate in store for C Camp, and thus had to arrange to have my family sent to some place far from here. He concurred and promised to help me.

That week two convoys of 3,000 prisoners were due to be sent from C Camp to western Germany's war plants. "These factories are the best setup," he said, "since the lodging and food do not aim at exterminating, but rather at the maintenance of good conditions for the workers, in order to assure maximum productivity."

I left a box of 100 cigarettes on his table. He accepted the package and promised that if my wife and daughter volunteered during the selection, he would assign them to one of the two convoys. I had got what I wanted. I hurried to C Camp, but there my job was even more difficult. I had to make my family understand that they had to get away from here. I could not tell them the truth, for I would only start a panic, which would be fatal for all of us. I asked for my wife and daughter in the overseer's little room, and tried to make them understand that, however painful it was for me, the situation demanded that they leave. They would have to renounce my help. For my part, I too would have to forgo the pleasure of seeing and helping them. Some time this week there would be a selection to fill a convoy quota. They were to volunteer for one of the convoys, preferably for the first. I explained to my wife that serious motives forced me to advise her thus; I asked her to tell all her acquaintances to volunteer as well for the convoys but that she say nothing more about it.

I might add that during the filling of work quotas, the SS commission first accepted volunteers for the convoys, and used arbitrary incorporation only when the number of volunteers did not attain the required number. Nevertheless, there were few volunteers, since nobody wanted to forsake the advantages of his present situation—that of not working—for another. Few were willing to volunteer for forced labor when the food rations were insufficient even to sustain life in the KZ. Poor, short-sighted women, if only they had understood the mentality of the Third Reich's KZ, they would have realized that those who did not work did not live.

My wife and daughter realized, however, that my reasons for making such a decision must be good, and they promised to volunteer for the initial quota. I made my good-byes, but told them I would return in two days to bring them some warm clothes and food for the journey.

When the two days were up, I returned to C Camp to bid them a last farewell, bringing the clothes and pro-

visions with me. But I did not return alone. I was afraid
to take such a load of packages through the C Camp gate.
Some high-ranking officers might have been in the neigh-
borhood when I arrived and become curious. So I asked
one of the crematorium SS guards, whom I had treated
for pleurisy, to come with me and help carry the packages. This time I did not visit my wife and daughter in
their barracks, but had them sent for from a deserted
point along the barbed wire enclosure. It was there we
held our last conversation. We threw the packages over
the barbed wire. The place was so out of the way that
nobody saw us. With the barbed wire strands separating
us, it was impossible even to kiss each other good-bye.

In the few minutes we spent together my wife assured
me that everything had worked out as planned. Both she
and our daughter had been accepted for the convoy, without having had to solicit the Oberschaarführer's help. I
was also happy to learn that many of the other women in
the camp had taken my wife's advice and volunteered for
the convoy.

26 THREE DAYS LATER I RETURNED TO C CAMP
to check and make certain my wife and
daughter had indeed departed. They were
gone all right, with one of the two convoys consisting of
3,000 prisoners. I did not know what the future might
hold in store for them, but I was nevertheless relieved,
for here they were headed towards certain death. Now,
with a little luck, they might escape with their lives. In-
dications that the war was drawing to a close were becoming increasingly evident. The Third Reich's grave was
already being dug. I had a feeling that, at this point in
the game, a prisoner's chances of survival were roughly
proportional to his distance from camps such as Auschwitz. Which meant that my own chances were growing
slimmer every day.

Whatever my fate, however, at least I could end my

days knowing that my family was now far from the paths leading to the funeral pyres. It was neither fear nor despair that kept the thought of death uppermost in my mind, but rather the memory of the eleventh Sonderkommando's bloody end, presaging our own, plus a coldly objective attitude, untainted by any sentimentality.

As I left C Camp, I let my gaze linger in farewell upon the rows of dilapidated barracks. It was with a mixture of sadness and compassion that I looked once more upon the grotesque spectacle of our women and girls: they who had once been so attractive, so meticulous in their toilet and dress, were now shaven and emaciated, dressed like scarecrows, stripped of all human dignity, ghosts of their former selves.

As I returned to the crematoriums I found myself shivering, and suddenly realized that autumn was here: it was already the end of September. The north wind, sweeping down from the already whitened summits of the mountains, sang through the barbed wires and made the shutters creak ominously. The only bird that inhabited this god-forsaken region, the crow, flashed against the leaden sky. From the crematoriums, built to endure forever, the wind bore clouds of smoke, and with them the characteristic, familiar odor of burning hair and flesh.

My days were spent in idleness, my nights were sleepless. I was terribly depressed; all desire had left me. Since my family's departure, I had been filled with loneliness and haunted by my own inactivity. For the past several days silence and boredom had weighed heavily on Auschwitz. A bad sign—and my intuition was just about infallible—merely the herald of more bloody deeds to come. The twelfth Sonderkommando had almost lived out its four months. The sands of our allotted time were fast running out. We had only a few days left—at most a week or two—to live.

Dr. Mengele's decision to liquidate C Camp had been carried out. Every evening fifty trucks brought the victims, 4,000 at a time, to the crematoriums. A horrible sight, this caravan of trucks, their headlights stabbing the darkness, each bearing a human cargo of eighty women who either filled the air with their screams or sat mute, paralyzed with fear. In slow succession the trucks rolled up and dumped the women, who had already been stripped of their clothes, at the top of the stairway leading down into the gas chamber. From there they were quickly pushed below. They all knew where they were going, but the rigors of their four months' captivity, the corporal punishment they had been made to endure, and the disintegration of their nervous systems, had reduced them to such a point that they were no longer capable of putting up any resistance, or even of feeling pain. They were herded passively into the gas chambers. Weary of being hunted and persecuted, of living in constant fear, they dumbly awaited the hand of the sure physician, Death. For them life had lost all meaning and purpose. To prolong it would merely have prolonged their suffering.

And what a long road they had traveled in coming here! How filled with unimaginable sorrow each lap of that journey! First, their warm, comfortable homes had been invaded and pillaged. Then, together with their husbands, children, and parents, they had been taken to the brick-kilns on the far edge of town, where for weeks they had been made to live and sleep in the swamps born of the spring rains. These were the "ghettos," from which, in small groups, they had been taken every day to the specially designed torture chambers, outfitted with all the latest instruments conducive to making people "talk." There they had been questioned, until, half dead with pain, they had confessed either the hiding place of their valuables, or the name of the person to whom they had confided them. Many had died from these interrogations. Those who survived had been almost relieved to find themselves being loaded into boxcars, eighty or ninety to a car, for it had meant they were leaving the torture chambers far behind. Or so they had thought. For four or five days they had lived in these cars, watching the dead pile up around them, till at last they reached the Jewish ramp of the Auschwitz concentration camp.

We already know what happened to them here. Heartbroken at being separated from their husbands and children, frantic with fear, sent, at "selection time," into the right-hand column, they at last reached C Camp. But before entering the foul, disease-ridden barracks, they were made to submit to another humiliation, designed to divest them of any lingering vestiges of human dignity: the baths. Ungentle hands cut their hair and stripped them of their clothes. After the bath they were given rags that no self-respecting beggar would ever have touched. In these clothes they received their first dividend under the Third Reich: lice.

After this reception, they began their life of confinement behind the KZ barbed wire, their life of the living dead. The food they received, more like dirty dishwater than anything else, was sufficient to keep them from dying, insufficient to keep them really alive. Albumin was completely lacking in their systems, causing their legs to become as heavy as lead. The absence of fats made their bodies swell. Their menstruations ceased. As a result, they became irritable and increasingly nervous, had migraines and nosebleeds. The lack of Vitamin B caused perpetual drowsiness and partial amnesia: often they could no longer remember the names of the streets where they had once lived, or their house numbers. Only their eyes were still alive, but even they no longer sparkled with intelligence.

These were the circumstances in which they submitted to the daily roll calls and musters, which lasted several hours. When they fainted and were rudely revived with a bucket of cold water, their eyes invariably turned towards the clouds of smoke that covered the KZ, or towards the flames belching from the crematorium stacks. These two signs, smoke and flames, reminded them, day and night, that they were living at the gate to the other world.

The C Camp inmates had lived for four months in the shadow of the crematorium gate: it took ten days for all of them to pass through it. Forty-five thousand tormented bodies rendered up their souls there. Upon C Camp, whose wire stands had enclosed as many poignant tragedies, a dismal silence descended.

27 THE SONDERKOMMANDO WAS AWAITING THE final blow. Day after day, week after week, month after month, terror had hovered over our heads, suspended by the thinnest of threads. And now, in a day or two, it would descend bringing with it instantaneous death, leaving in its wake only a pile of silvery

ashes. We were ready for it. Hourly we awaited the arrival of our SS executioners.

Early in the morning of October 6th, 1944, a shot rang out from one of the watch towers, killing a KZ prisoner who had strayed outside the neutral zone into the area between the first and second lines of guards that surrounded the camp. The prisoner, an ex-Russian officer, had been sent here for trying to escape from a prisoner-of-war camp. In all probability he had been trying to escape again when the guard had fired on him.

A political commission headed by Dr. Mengele proceeded to the spot to make the customary investigation. If the victim had been Jewish his body would have been shipped directly to the morgue and thence to the crematoriums, and that would have been the end of the matter. But since this was a Russian officer, whose name and personal data were duly inscribed in the camp records, the same procedure could not be followed. An autopsy report would be required to explain his death. Following his on-the-spot investigation, Dr. Mengele had the body taken to the crematorium, with orders that an autopsy be made. The report was to be ready by 2:30 P.M. Dr. Mengele would pick it up and check the findings by personally examining the body.

It was 9:00 A.M. when Dr. Mengele left the dissecting room. I had the body placed on the table, and would have completed the autopsy in thirty or forty minutes if the date had not been October 6th, the last day but one of the Sonderkommando's allotted life span. We were not certain of anything, but I felt the imminence of death.

Since I was unable to work, I left the dissecting room and went to my room, planning to take a healthy dose of sleeping tablets. I smoked cigarette after cigarette, my nerves completely shot. Unable to stay put, I crossed into the incineration room, where I found the Sonderkommando crew working half-heartedly, despite the fact that several hundred bodies were stacked up in front of the ovens. Small groups had formed and the men were talking in whispers. I went upstairs to the kommando's living quarters and immediately noticed that something was amiss. Normally, after morning muster and breakfast, the night shift turned in. Now, however, at 10 o'clock, everyone was still up. I also noticed that they were dressed in sport clothes, with sweaters and boots, although the room was bright with a warm October sun. Here too, many of the men were huddled, talking in whispers, while others moved about feverishly, arranging and packing their clothes in suitcases. It was obvious that some sort of plot was being hatched. But what? I entered the small room that housed the kommando chief and found the various leaders of the night shift seated around the table: the engineer, the mechanic, the head chauffeur and the chief of the gas kommando. No sooner had I taken my seat when the kommando chief took an almost empty bottle from the table and poured me a large glass of brandy. It was a strong Polish eau-de-vie, the famous cumin brandy. I downed my glass in one gulp. Now, in the waning hours of the Sonderkommando's fourth month, it might not be a life-prolonging elixir, but it was none the less an excellent remedy for dulling the fear of death. My comrades presented me with a detailed account of our situation. All evidence seemed to indicate that the Sonderkommando's liquidation would not take place before the following day, and perhaps the day after. But careful plans had been made for the 860 members of the kommando to try and force their way out of the camp. The break was scheduled for that night.

Once out, we would head for the loop of the Vistula two kilometers away. At this time of year the river was very low and could easily be forded. Eight kilometers from the Vistula there were vast forests, extending to the Polish border, in which we should be able to live for weeks, even months if necessary, in relative safety. Or perhaps we would run into some partisans along the way. Our supply of weapons was adequate. During the preceding few days a shipment of about a hundred boxes of high explosives had reached the camp, sent from the Unio factories of Auschwitz, a munitions plant that employed Polish Jews as workers. The Germans used it for blowing up railroad lines. Besides this stock, we had five machine guns and twenty hand grenades.

"This should suffice," said one of the group. "With the element of surprise on our side, we can disarm the guards using only our revolvers. Then we'll take the SS by surprise in their dormitories and force them to come with us until we have no further use for them."

The signal to attack would be given by flashlight signals from number one crematorium. Number two would immediately transmit the signal to number three, which would in turn alert number four. The plans seemed all the more feasible to me for the simple reason that the only crematorium working was number one. And even it would knock off work at 6:00 P.M., which meant that the Sonderkommando night shift would not go on duty that evening. Whenever this happened, the SS guards tended to relax their vigil. There were three SS guards in each crematorium.

We adjourned the meeting until the evening, the order being that, until the moment the signal was given, everyone should accomplish his task as usual, scrupulously avoiding any act liable to arouse suspicion.

Returning to my room, I again passed through the oven room. The men seemed to be working even more slowly than before. I informed my two colleagues of the plan, but refrained from mentioning it to the lab assistant. He would inevitably be drawn into it once it began, but I saw no need to inform him of it for the present.

Time moved forward on leaden feet. Lunch time arrived. We ate slowly, then went into the crematorium courtyard to warm ourselves in the slanting rays of the autumn sun. I noticed that the SS guards were nowhere to be seen. But there was probably nothing unusual about that; it had happened more than once before. They were no doubt in their rooms. The gates were closed. Outside, the camp SS on duty were at their posts. So I accorded no importance to the absence of guards inside. I smoked my cigarette in peace. To know that within a few hours we would be outside these barbed wires and free again lifted a dark cloud from my mind, a cloud that had hovered there since my first day in the KZ. Even if the attempt failed, I would have lost nothing.

I looked at my watch. Half past one. I got up and asked my colleagues to join me for the autopsy, so we could be ready with the report when Dr. Mengele arrived to pick it up. They followed me silently into the dissecting room, and we began the autopsy immediately. Today one of my associates was performing the dissection, while I recorded his findings on my typewriter.

We had been working for about 20 minutes when a tremendous explosion rocked the walls. In the echoing silence, the steady staccato of machine gun fire reached our ears. Peering through the green mosquito netting

that covered the main window, I saw the red-tiled roof
and supporting beams of number three crematorium blow
off, followed by an immense spiral of flame and black
smoke. No more than a minute later, machine gun fire
broke out just in front of the dissecting room door. We
had no idea what had happened. Our plans called for to-
night. Two possibilities occurred to me: either someone
had betrayed us, thus enabling the SS to step in and break
up the planned escape, or else a considerable force of
partisans had attacked the camp. The dismal wail of sirens
began in both Auschwitz I and Auschwitz II. The explo-
sions grew louder and louder, and the rattle of submachine
guns more and more persistent. Then we could hear the
harsher staccato of field machine guns. I had already made
up my mind what to do. Whether it was a question of
treason or of a partisan attack, it seemed best for the
moment to remain in the dissecting room and see how
the situation evolved. From the window I saw 80 to 100
trucks arriving. The first one pulled up in front of our
crematorium. Half a company jumped out and formed
up in battle formation in front of the barbed wire fences.

I began to see what had happened. The Sonderkommando men had taken possession of number one crematorium and, from every window and door, were spray-
ing the SS troops with bullets and grenades. Their defense
seemed effective, for I saw several soldiers drop, either
dead or wounded. Seeing this, the besiegers decided to
resort to more drastic methods. They brought up 50 well-
trained police dogs and unleashed them on the Sonderkommando entrenched behind the walls of number one.
But for some strange reason these dogs usually so fero-
cious and obedient, refused to budge: ears back, tails between their legs, they took shelter behind their SS masters.
Perhaps it was because the dogs had been trained to deal
with prisoners wearing striped burlap, whereas the Sonderkommando never wore this "uniform." Or perhaps, too
long used to dealing with weakened, unarmed prisoners,
they were momentarily frightened by the smell of powder
and scorched flesh, the noise and confusion of a pitched
battle. In any case, the SS soon realized their mistake and,
without letting up on their fire, began to haul some howitzers into position.

It was impossible for the Sonderkommando to hold out
against such numerical and material odds. Shouting ex-

ultantly, they erupted through the back gates of the crematorium. Firing as they went, they poured through the electrified barbed wires that had been cut ahead of time, and headed for the loop of the Vistula.

For about ten minutes the fighting was heavy on both sides. Loud machine gun fire from the watch towers mingled with the lesser blasts of the sub-machine guns, and interspersed could be heard the explosion of hand grenades and dynamite. Then, as suddenly as it had begun, everything became quiet.

Then the SS stationed in front of the crematorium advanced, leaving behind the two howitzers, which they had not used. With fixed bayonets, they attacked the building from all sides, and scattered through the rooms in the basement and ground floor. A group of SS entered the dissecting room. Guns leveled, they surrounded us and drove us, under a rain of blows, into the courtyard. There they made us lie down on our bellies, our faces hard against the ground. The order rang out: "Anyone who makes a move, or raises his head, will get a bullet in the back of the neck!" A few minutes later I could tell from the sound of footsteps that another SS group had rounded up and brought back a considerable number of Sonderkommando men. They too were made to lie down beside us. How many of them could there be? With my head pressed against the ground it was impossible to tell for sure. Three or four minutes later another group arrived and was made to lie down behind us.

While we were lying there inert on the ground, a hail of kicks and blows from the guards' clubs fell on our heads, shoulders and backs. I could feel the warm blood trickling down my face, till its salty taste reached my tongue. But only the first blows really hurt me. My head was spinning, my ears were ringing, my mind was a blank. I could no longer feel anything. I had the impression I was slipping into the indifference that precedes death.

For some twenty or thirty minutes we lay on the ground waiting for the bullet from the SS guards standing behind us. In this position, I knew it was with a bullet in the head that they intended to kill us. The swiftest of deaths at least, and in these circumstances the least horrible. In my mind I imagined my head blown off under the tremendous impact of the bullet fired point-blank, my skull exploding into a thousand pieces.

Suddenly I heard the sound of a car. It must be Dr. Mengele, I thought. The political SS were awaiting his arrival. I didn't dare lift my head to look, but I recognized his voice. An order, from the lips of an SS: "Doctors, on your feet!" All four of us got up and stood at attention, waiting for what would follow. Dr. Mengele made a sign for us to approach. My face and shirt were bloody, my clothes covered with mud as I appeared before him. Three high-ranking SS officers were standing beside him. Dr. Mengele asked us what part we had played in all this.

"No part," I replied, "unless carrying out the orders of the Hauptsturmführer could be construed as guilt. We were dissecting the body of the Russian officer when the incident occurred. It was the explosion that interrupted our dissection. The unfinished autopsy report is still in the typewriter. We did not leave our posts and were there when they found us."

The SS commander confirmed our words. Dr. Mengele looked hard at me and said: "Go wash up and return to your work."

I turned and left, followed by my three companions. We had got no more than twenty steps when a burst of machine guns sounded behind us. The Sonderkommando's life was over.

I did not look back; on the contrary, I increased my pace and returned to my room. I tried to roll a cigarette but my hands were shaking too much and kept tearing the paper. Finally I got one rolled, lighted it, inhaled deeply several times, and, on unsteady legs, made for my bed and lay down. Only then did I begin to feel the aches and bruises that racked my whole body, the result of the SS kicks and blows.

So much had happened today, and yet it was only 3:00 P.M. The fact that I had come away with my life gave me neither comfort nor joy. I knew it was only a reprieve. I knew Dr. Mengele, and I knew the mentality of the SS. I was also fully cognizant of the importance of my work: for the moment I was indispensable. Besides myself, there was no physician in the KZ qualified to meet Dr. Mengele's requirements. And even if there were, they would be careful not to reveal themselves and make public their professional abilities, for to do so would be to fall into Dr. Mengele's hands, and so bring their lives to an end: like every member of the Sonderkommando, they too would find themselves condemned to a life span of four months.

When my nerves became calmer, I got up and went to look around. I wanted to know exactly what had happened this afternoon. Was there really a traitor among us? And did the SS really suppress the revolt by destroying the Sonderkommando? Even if they had been hunting for a pretext, they could never have found a better reason to liquidate the kommando. It was quite likely that today merely marked the expiration of our allotted four months, and the SS had received orders to liquidate us. They had probably set out to execute their orders, but had discovered, to their surprise, that the twelfth Sonderkommando had no intention of lining up in the courtyard. Nor were they to be lured by the pretext that this assembly was merely to make some routine announcement, or for muster. Our kommando, quite aware that the SS had come to exterminate us, had chosen to go down fighting.

Now my comrades were lying naked in long rows, in front of the cremation ovens. One after the other I identified the bodies of those I knew; at least they had died believing that freedom was only around the corner. They had been brought back on pushcarts from the spot where they had fallen, somewhere inside the outer line of guards. Those who had been executed in the courtyard as we were walking away were also here. After all resistance had been crushed, the bodies had been removed from number two, three and four crematoriums and brought for cremation to number one, which was manned by thirty new, hastily recruited Sonderkommando men.

I found myself standing beside an SS noncom, who was busy recording the tattoo numbers of the dead. Without my asking, he informed me that twelve Sonder men were still missing. Of the others, all but seven were dead. Those seven were myself and my two associates, the lab assistant, the engineer in charge of the dynamos and ventilators, the head chauffeur, and the "Pipel," that is, a jack-of-all-trades assigned to the SS personnel, whose duties included taking care of their clothes and boots, cleaning their kitchen and answering the phone. It was he who gave me a detailed account of the day's events. It had not been a case of treason. Here is the "Pipel's" tale:

At 2:00 P.M. a truckload of political SS arrived at

number three crematorium. Their commander ordered
the Sonderkommando to assemble, but no one moved.
He must have had an inkling of what was brewing. In
any event, he apparently figured he would get better results if he tried lying to the Sonderkommando, and God
knows the SS were past masters in the art of lying. Stopping in the center of the courtyard, he gave a short speech,
worthy of the SS:

"Men," he shouted, "you have worked here long enough.
By orders of my superiors, you are to be sent in a convoy
to a rest camp. There you will be given good clothes,
you'll have plenty to eat, and your life will be easier.
Those whose tattoo numbers I call out, step forward and
line up."

Then he began the roll call. He first called out the
numbers of the Hungarian members of number three
Sonderkommando, 100 in all. The KZ's "youngest" prisoners, they lined up without further protest. More fear
than courage was visible in their expressions. A detachment of SS immediately took charge of them and removed
them from the courtyard, then marched them to D Camp
and crammed them into Barracks 13.

Meanwhile, in number three crematorium, roll call continued. Now it was the turn of the Greeks, who failed to
show a similar alacrity in lining up, but nevertheless
obeyed. Next, a group of Poles. Grumbles and muttered
protests swelled to a surly roar. The SS called another
number. Silence; no one moved. When the officer raised
his head and frowned a bottle of mineral water fell at his
feet and exploded. Seven SS, including the group commander, fell dead or wounded. The bottle had been thrown
by one of the Poles. The SS opened a deadly fire on the
rioters, who retreated and took up defensive positions
inside the crematorium. Thus protected, they began tossing
other explosive-filled bottles into the courtyard. A burst
of machine-gun fire from some of the SS mowed down the
Greeks, who were still lined up in the courtyard. A few
tried to escape, but were killed as they reached the gate.

Without letting up on their fire, the SS moved in towards the crematorium entrance. It was no easy job, for
the Poles put up a stout defense. Their cascade of bottles
succeeded in keeping the SS at a respectful distance. Just
then, a tremendous explosion rocked the area, felling
those attackers who had moved in close to the building.

The crematorium roof blew off, sending a shower of beams and shingles flying in all directions, while smoke and flames billowed skyward. Four drums of gasoline had exploded, reducing the building to rubble and burying the Sonderkommando men inside. A few of those who escaped with their lives tried to carry on the fight, but the SS machine guns made short work of them. Others, wounded but still able to walk, headed towards the door with their hands up, but another burst tumbled them as well. They expected what they got, but fire was gutting the building and they chose the easier death. At the same time, the hundred Hungarians were hastily returned to the court-yard and executed on the spot.

Thus the riot began in number three. In number one, work continued as usual till number three exploded. The sound of the explosion brought the tension, already at a high pitch from the wait, to a paroxysm. No one knew exactly what happened during the first few minutes. The men working at the ovens left their posts and gathered at the far end of the room, where they tried to figure out what was going on and what steps to take.

They did not have long to puzzle, however, for the SS guard came over and asked who had given them per-mission to stop work and leave the ovens. Apparently the work boss's reply failed to satisfy him, for he dealt the man a withering blow on the head with the curved end of his cane—each of the SS guards carried one, the better to encourage the Sonder men in their work Ru-mor had it that a second Sonder man also had his head split open by the same cane. But the work boss, the toughest man in the kommando, was only staggered by the blow. His face was covered with blood, but he was still on his feet. He quickly drew a sharp knife from the top of his boot and thrust it into the guard's chest. As the guard fell two alert members of the kommando grabbed him, opened the door of the nearest oven, and shoved him headfirst into the flames.

The whole incident happened in the space of a few seconds, but another SS guard, drawn by the crowd, ap-parently arrived just in time to see the booted feet disap-pear into the oven. He knew it could only have been a Sonder man or an SS guard, but before he had time to learn which, one of the Sonder crew floored him with a sharp uppercut. With the help of a buddy, he shoved the second SS guard in beside the first.

After that it took only a few seconds to break out the machine guns, hand grenades and boxes of dynamite. Firing broke out, the SS stationed at one end of the room, the Sonderkommando at the other. A hand grenade tossed into the midst of the SS killed seven and wounded a number of others. Several kommando men were also killed or wounded, and the situation of the survivors was becoming increasingly desperate. But when a few more SS dropped, the remainder, about 20 in all, took to their heels and ran for the crematorium door. There they were met by reinforcements, more than enough to turn the tide of battle in their favor.

The rest was history. Seven of us were left in the crematoriums. The twelve fugitives were rounded up during the night. They had succeeded in crossing the Vistula, but were completely worn out and had sought shelter in a house they thought might furnish them with at least a temporary hiding place. But the owner had informed an SS detachment combing the area, and all twelve had been ambushed and recaptured.

I was already in bed, almost asleep, when a new burst of machine-gun fire roused me from my state of semi-consciousness. A few minutes later heavy footsteps echoed in the hallway. My door opened and two SS staggered in, their faces covered with blood.

The twelve prisoners had attacked the patrol that had brought them back to the crematorium courtyard, in a desperate effort to seize their weapons. The twelve had had only their fists to fight with; the result had been swift and sure: all twelve had been quickly killed. But they had succeeded in badly mauling the SS guards, who now asked me to treat their wounds. I mutely carried out their orders.

The loss of these twelve companions was a terrible blow to me. After so much effort and loss of life, still no one had succeeded in escaping to tell the world the full story of this hellish prison.

Later I learned that news of the revolt had nevertheless reached the outside world. Some of the KZ prisoners related the story to the civilians who worked with them. And besides, the tongues of certain SS guards were said to have wagged.

It was indeed an historic event, the first of its kind since the founding of the KZ. Eight hundred and fifty-three prisoners, and seventy SS were killed. Included among the latter were an Obersturmführer, seventeen Oberschaarführer and Schaarfuhrer and fifty-two Sturmmänner. Number three crematorium burned to the ground. And number four, as a result of damage to its equipment, was rendered useless.

28 I AWOKE DEPRESSED AFTER A NIGHT OF troubled sleep. My nerves were more shot than ever: even my colleagues' whispered conversation, the sound of their footsteps, grated on me like sandpaper.

I was in a foul mood as I went with my associates once again into the dissecting room. En route we had to cross the incineration room. The unfriendly concrete floor extended to the very edge of the ovens. They had finished the job of cremating our comrades by midnight last night. The cooling ovens gave off a feeble warmth. The thirty new Sonder men, stricken by the tragedy they had been made to witness on the day of their arrival, were sitting or lying in deadly silence on the beds of the deceased.

But this condition lasted for only a few days. Life soon resumed its normal course, as evidenced by their desire for a good meal and cigarettes, and especially for brandy, the blessed remedy of all Sonderkommando men, the panacea for crematorium sickness. After having gone without clothes in the KZ barracks, they enjoyed the comfort of decent ones. Personal hygiene was once again a reality: showers, plenty of water and soap, towels in abundance. I watched them as an old sergeant might watch a group of new recruits. They would get used to all this before long.

In the dissecting room, for lack of something better to do—*ut aliquid videatur*—I invented some jobs to keep my colleagues occupied. I had them clean the surgical instruments till they shone like display pieces, then sort them and put them away. The mosquito netting, after the battle of the previous day, was also in need of repair. As for myself, I was seated at the table, my head swathed in bandages and adhesive tape, mentally compiling a list of complaints and requests I wanted to present to Dr. Mengele at the earliest possible opportunity.

For one thing, I planned to tell him that none of the crematorium rooms was suitable as a dissecting room, for the simple reason that, no matter where you happened to be here, you could not escape the heart-rending screams of the deported on their way to death, screams that pierced to the very marrow of your bones. Whether it was the gas chamber or a bullet in the neck, the screams were the same. It was impossible for me to concentrate properly on my work here. Since the day of my arrival, when I had learned the fate of the eleven preceding kommandos, I had lived in a world of constant dread: four months of nerve-racking tension, waiting, day by day, for the moment when our kommando would meet with the same fate.

I also planned to ask him to be lenient with my work in the future if it proved to be inaccurate. Why? Because, no later than yesterday, October 6th, 1944, when I had been ordered to perform an autopsy on the body of a Russian officer and to prepare the dissection report, number three crematorium had blown up before my eyes, and we had been attacked by a battalion of SS troops. Howitzers had been brought up and police dogs unleashed against us. Hand grenades had exploded around us. SS soldiers, with fixed bayonets, had charged into this so-called scientific institute I was supposed to direct and run us into the courtyard, striking and kicking us as we went. Then we had been made to lie down in the mud. I had come within a hair's breadth of being transformed from a coroner into a subject for dissection myself. It was true that Dr. Mengele had saved me from this fate and rescued me from the rows of the damned, but only to be returned to this house of sorrow for a new reprieve of four months. I would ask him to admit, frankly, what an impossible situation ours had been yesterday afternoon and evening. For even after the worst was over, I had yet had to give first aid to two SS noncoms who five hours earlier had kicked and struck me unmercifully and then waited, their guns aimed at my head, for the signal to pull the trigger.

Such were the complaints I intended making to my

chief. But principally I wanted to prevail upon him to have the dissecting room and its personnel transferred to some place in the KZ better suited to research.

Just as I reached this point in my musings, Dr. Mengele opened the door. As the rules prescribed, I rose and came to attention and, as the senior member present, announced: "Captain, three doctors and one lab assistant at their posts."

He looked quizzically at my bandaged head.

"What happened to you?" he asked with an enigmatic smile that seemed half-serious, half-joking. The nature of his question gave me the impression that he would have liked to pretend that yesterday's events had never occurred. So I did not answer him. My list of complaints withered, till only the one obsessing request remained.

"Captain," I said unconvincingly, "this environment is highly unsuitable for scientific research. Wouldn't it be possible to transfer the dissecting room to a better place?"

He looked at me steadily, his expression hardening. "What's wrong?" he said coldly. "Getting sentimental?"

I regretted having let myself go, having momentarily forgotten the discretion I usually displayed in his presence. I had dared criticize the one place, the one environment where my soft-brained superior really felt at home: the blazing glow of the pyres and the spiraling smoke of the crematorium stacks; the air heavy with the odor of burning bodies; the walls resounding with the screams of the damned and the metallic rattle of machine guns fired pointblank; it was to this that the demented doctor came for rest and relaxation after each selection, after each display of "fireworks." This was where he spent all his free time; here, in this man-made hell, the fiendish physician of Auschwitz made me cut open the bodies of hundreds of freshly murdered people, whose flesh was also used for the cultivation of bacteria in an electric incubator. Obsessed with the belief that he had been chosen to discover the cause of multiple births, here, within these bloodstained walls, Dr. Mengele sat hunched for hours at a time over his microscopes.

Today, however, I noticed that he appeared tired. He had just come from the Jewish unloading platform, where he had stood for hours in a biting rain, selecting the inhabitants of the Riga ghetto. As usual, though, "selection"

was no longer a very applicable term, for everyone had
been sent to the left. Both crematoriums still in operation
were full, as was the immense pyre ditch. To cope with
this new influx the ranks of the new Sonderkommando had
been increased to 460 men.

Dr. Mengele approached the table without bothering
to take off his coat and kepi, which were soaked through.
In fact he did not even seem to notice them.

"Captain," I said, "let me take your hat and coat into
the oven room. They'll be dry in five minutes."

"Never mind," he replied, "the water won't get any
farther than my skin anyway."

He asked to see the dissection report on the Russian
officer. I handed it to him and he began to read. After
reading three or four lines he handed it back to me.

"I'm very tired," he said. "You read it." But after I
had proceeded only a few lines he interrupted me again.
"Let it go," he said, "that won't be necessary." And his
gaze wandered to the window, out of which he stared
absently.

What could have happened to this man? Could it be
that he had had enough of all this horror? Or had he received some bad news informing him that henceforth all
this was meaningless? It was also possible that the strain
of the preceding months had at last begun to take its toll.

During our numerous contacts and talks together, Dr.
Mengele had never granted me what I might call a private
conversation. But now, seeing him so depressed, I screwed
up my courage. "Captain," I said, "when is all this destruction going to cease?"

He looked at me and replied: *"Mein Freund! Es geht
immer weiter, immer weiter!* My friend, it goes on and
on, on and on . . ." His words seemed to betray a note
of silent resignation.

He got up from his chair and left the laboratory, his
briefcase in his hand. I accompanied him to his car.

"During the next few days you'll have some interesting work," he said, and with these words he climbed into
his car and drove away.

I shuddered at the thought. No doubt this "interesting
work" meant a new group of twins.

29 THE CREMATORIUMS WERE BEING READIED. The men of the Sonderkommando were redoing the refractory surfaces of the furnace entrances, painting the heavy iron doors and oiling the hinges. The dynamos and ventilators were running all day long. A specialist made sure they were functioning properly. The arrival of the Litzmannstadt ghetto had been announced.

This ghetto, it should be noted, was established by the Germans in 1939. In the beginning it had housed some 500,0000 souls, who worked in enormous war factories. In exchange for their work, they were paid in "ghetto Marks," but only in sufficient quantities to buy a meager supply of food. Needless to say, the difference between the work effort furnished and the food consumed resulted in a high mortality rate. Numerous epidemics also decimated their ranks. Thus, by the fall of 1944, only 70,000 of the original half million were left.

And now the fatal hour had arrived for these remaining few. They arrived at the Jewish ramp in groups of 10,000. The selection sent 95 per cent to the left, only 5 per cent to the right.

Persecuted and tortured, physically and morally broken by five years of ghetto life, bowed by the knowledge of their accursed race's tragic destiny, aged by forced labor, they arrived completely apathetic. Although they realized as they crossed the threshold of the crematorium that they were entering upon the last lap of their lives, there was an air of indifference about them.

I descended into the undressing room. Their clothes and shoes were strewn about the floor. But then, it would have been difficult to hang on coat hangers these scraps of leather and wood that passed for shoes. Nor did the cloakroom number they were assigned arouse their interest. They set their hand luggage down anywhere they happened to be. The men of the Sonderkommando whose job it was to sort their belongings opened a few packages and showed me their contents: a few biscuits made of corn flour, water and a bit of linseed oil, and, in some cases, three or four pounds of oatmeal; that was all they had.

When the convoys arrived, Dr. Mengele espied, among those lined up for selection, a hunchbacked man about fifty years old. He was not alone; standing beside him was a tall, handsome boy of fifteen or sixteen. The latter, however, had a deformed right foot, which had been corrected by an apparatus made of a metal plate and an orthopedic, thick-soled shoe. They were father and son. Dr. Mengele thought he had discovered, in the person of the hunchback father and his lame son, a sovereign example to demonstrate his theory of the Jewish race's degeneracy. He had them fall out of ranks immediately. Taking his notebook, he inscribed something in it, and entrusted the two wretches to the care of an SS trooper, who took them to number one crematorium.

It was around noon. Number one was not working that day. Having nothing to do for the moment, I was in my room idling away the time. The SS soldier on duty came in and asked me to report to the gate. The father and son, accompanied by the SS guard, were already there. I took the message sent me, which read: "Dissecting room, number one crematorium: that these two men be examined from a clinical point of view; that exact measurements of the two men be made; that clinical records be set up including all interesting details, and most especially those relative to the causes which provoked the bodily deformities."

A second note was enclosed for Oberschaarführer Mussfeld. Even without reading it I knew what it said. I entrusted it for transmission to a Sonder man.

Father and son—their faces wan from their miserable years in the Litzmannstadt ghetto—were filled with forebodings. They looked at me questioningly. I took them across the courtyard, which at this hour of the day was filled with sunlight. On our way to the dissecting room I reassured them with a few well-chosen words. Luckily there were no corpses on the dissecting table; it would have indeed been a horrible sight for them to come upon.

To spare them I decided not to conduct the examination in the austere dissecting room, which reeked with the odor of formaldehyde, but in the pleasant, well-lighted study hall. From our conversation, I learned that the father had been a respected citizen of Litzmannstadt, a wholesaler in cloth. During the years of peace between wars he had often taken his son with him on his business trips to Vienna, to have him examined and treated by the most famous specialists.

I first examined the father in detail, omitting nothing. The deviation of his spinal column was the result of retarded rickets. In spite of a most thorough examination, I discovered no symptom of any other illness.

I tried to console him by saying that he would probably be sent to a work camp.

Before proceeding to the examination of the boy I conversed with him at some length. He had a pleasant face, an intelligent look, but his morale was badly shaken. Trembling with fear, he related in an expressionless voice the sad, painful, sometimes terrible events which had marked his five years in the ghetto. His mother, a frail and sensitive creature, had not been able to long endure the ordeals which had befallen her. She had become melancholic and depressed. For weeks on end she had eaten almost nothing, so that her son and husband might have a little more food. A true wife and Jewish mother, who had loved her own to the point of madness, she had died a martyr during the first year of her life in the ghetto. So it was that they had lived in the ghetto, the father without his wife, the son without his mother.

And now they were in number one crematorium. Once again I was struck by the horrible irony of the situation. I, a Jewish doctor, had to examine them with exact clinical methods before they died, and then perform the dissection on their still warm bodies. So shaken was I by the situation, about which I was powerless to do anything at all, that I suddenly felt myself spinning close to the edge of madness. By whose will had such evil, such a succession of horrors been made to descend upon our wretched people? Could this be the will of God? No; I could not believe it.

By an immense effort of self-control I got hold of myself and examined the boy. On his right foot I noticed a congenital deformity; some of the muscles were lacking.

The medical term used to describe this deformity is

hypomyelia. I could see that extremely expert hands had
practiced several operations on him, but as a result one
foot was shorter than the other. With a bandage and
orthopedic socks, however, he could walk perfectly well.
I saw no other deformity to be indicated.

I askd them if they wanted something to eat.

"We haven't had anything to eat for some time,"
they told me.

I called a man from the Sonderkommando and had
some food brought for them: a plate of stewed beef and
macaroni, a dish not to be found outside the confines of
the Sonderkommando. They began to eat ravenously,
unaware that this was their "Last Supper."

Scarcely half an hour later Oberschaarführer Mussfeld appeared with four Sonderkommando men. They
took the two prisoners into the furnace room and had
them undress. Then the Ober's revolver cracked twice.
Father and son were stretched out on the concrete, covered with blood, dead. Oberschaarführer Mussfeld had
faithfully executed Dr. Mengele's orders.

Now it was my turn again. The two bodies were
brought back into the dissecting room. So sickened was
I by what had just happened that I entrusted the dissection to my associates and confined myself to recording
the data. The dissection revealed nothing more than I
had previously ascertained in my *in vivo* examination.
The cases were banal, but could nevertheless very easily
be utilized as propaganda in support of the Third Reich's
theory concerning the degeneracy of the Jewish race.

Late in the afternoon, already having sent at least
10,000 men to their death, Dr. Mengele arrived. He
listened attentively to my report concerning both the
in vivo and *post mortem* observations made on the two
victims.

"These bodies must not be cremated," he said. "They
must be prepared and their skeletons sent to the Anthropological Museum in Berlin. What systems do you know
for the preparations of skeletons?"

"There are two methods," I said. "The first consists
of immersing the bodies in lime chloride, which con-
sumes all the soft parts in about two weeks' time. Then
the bodies are immersed in a gasoline bath, which dis-
solves all the fat and makes the skeletons dry, odorless
and white. Then there's a second method: by cooking.

What you do there is boil the bodies in water until the flesh can easily be stripped from the bones. Then the same gasoline bath is applied." Dr. Mengele ordered me to use the quickest method: by cooking.

In the KZ orders were always cursory. How the prisoners should go about procuring materials necessary for their execution was never specified. The order had to be carried out, and that was as much as was known. I was therefore faced with a serious problem: what could I have the bodies cooked in? I put the question to Oberschaarführer Mussfeld. I told him that I had two bodies that had to be cooked, but that I didn't have any. . . .

Even he was horrified by my tale. He thought for a minute, then remembered that there were two iron casks in the courtyard which were generally used in the storehouse. He put them at my disposal and advised me to place them on bricks in the courtyard and to light an open fire beneath them.

The base was prepared, and the two casks, containing the bodies, placed upon it. Two Sonderkommando men were given the job of gathering wood and keeping the fire hot. After five hours, I tested the bodies and found that the soft parts were now easily separable from the bones. I ordered the fire to be put out, but the casks had to stay there until they cooled.

Having nothing else to do, I remained seated beneath a little arbor not far from the casks. A deep silence surrounded me. Some prisoner-masons were in the process of repairing the crematory chimneys. Dusk was falling. The casks ought to be cold by now. I was just about to have them emptied when one of my men came running up to me and said: "Doctor, hurry, the Poles are eating the meat in the casks!"

I took off as fast as my legs could carry me. Four men, dressed in the striped jerkin of prisoners, were standing beside the casks, struck dumb with horror. They were the Polish masons I had noticed earlier. They had finished their work and were waiting in the courtyard for their guards to come and take them back to Auschwitz I. Starved, they had been scrounging for some food when by chance they had come upon the casks, which had been left unguarded for a few minutes. Thinking it was the Sonderkommando meat which was being cooked, they had sniffed at it, then fetched up some pieces of flesh which were not covered with skin and begun to eat them.

They had not gotten very far, however, for the two Sonderkommando men detailed to supervise the cooking and watch the casks had seen what was happening and hurried back. When they learned what kind of meat it was they had been eating, the Poles were sick, horrified, paralyzed. . .

After the gasoline bath, the lab assistant very completely gathered up the bones of the skeletons and placed them on the same work table where, the evening before, I had examined the still living men.

Dr. Mengele was highly pleased. He had brought several fellow officers with him. They pompously examined certain parts of the skeletons and launched into high-sounding, scientific terms, talking as if the two victims represented an extremely rare medical phenomenon. They abandoned themselves completely to their pseudoscience.

And yet, far from being an extraordinary abnormality, it is common to hundreds of thousands of men of all races and climates. Even a doctor whose practice is limited has often come across it. But these two cases could, by their very nature, be exploited as useful propaganda. Nazi propaganda never hesitated to clothe its monstrous lies in scientific apparel. The method often worked too, since those towards whom these lies were directed usually had little or no critical faculty, and accepted as fact everything which bore the regime's stamp of approval.

The skeletons were wrapped in large sacks of strong paper, and forwarded to Berlin, marked: "Urgent: National Defense." I was relieved that they were finally out of my sight, for they had caused me many bitter hours, both while they were still alive and afterward.

At the end of a week's time, the liquidation of the Litzmannstadt ghetto had been completed. A cold autumn rain replaced the sun that had warmed the waning days of October. Fog and mist shrouded the KZ barracks; my past and future also dissolved, as in a sea of mist. The rain continued for several days, and the wet cold, that penetrated to the bone, made my bitterness all the more acute. Everywhere I went, everywhere I looked, I saw only electrified barbed wires to remind me how vain it was to hope.

On the third day following the liquidation of the Litzmannstadt ghetto, the head of the Sonderkommando brought in a woman and two children, drenched to the skin and shivering with the cold. They had escaped when the last convoy had been sent to its death. Guessing what was in store for them, they had hidden behind the piles of wood that were used for heating and that, for lack of a better place, were stored in the courtyard. Their convoy had disappeared, swallowed by the earth before their very eyes. And no one had ever returned. Numb with fear and cold, they had waited there for some miraculous turn of fate to deliver them. But nothing had happened. For three days they had hidden in the rain and cold, with nothing to eat, their rags scant protection against the elements, till finally the Sonderkommando chief had found them, almost unconscious, while making his rounds. Unable to help them in any way, he had taken them to the Oberschaarführer.

The woman, who was about 30 but who looked closer to 50, had gathered her waning forces and thrown herself at Mussfeld's feet, begging him to spare her life and those of her ten- and twelve-year-old children. She had worked for five years in a clothing factory in the ghetto, she said, making uniforms for the German army. She was still willing to work, to do anything, if only they would let her live.

All this was quite useless. Here there was no salvation. They had to die. Yet the KZ's past must also have had its effect on the *Ober;* he sent another man in his place to perform the murder.

30 THAT WAS ANOTHER LITTLE EPISODE WE forgot, for it was absolutely necessary to forget it if we wanted to keep from going mad. Darkness before and darkness behind. . . .

As always, drink was a great help, a momentary but necessary respite. When I thought of the past, it often seemed to me that all this was merely a horrible dream. My only desire was to forget everything, to think of nothing.

It was now November, 1944. Snow was falling in big flakes, veiling everything in a swirl of white. The watch towers were barely visible, vague fingers of gray rising above us. The wind sang even louder in the barbed wires, and still the only birds to darken the sky were the crows.

I went for a short walk before nightfall. The weather was hardly conducive, but the cold wind was invigorating, soothing my tired nerves. I made several turns around the courtyard; my steps took me past the stairway leading down into the gas chambers. I paused there for a few seconds, remembering that today was All Saints' Day. A deadly silence brooded over Auschwitz. The cold concrete steps descended and dissolved into darkness. These same steps where four million people, guilty of no crime, had bade life good-bye and descended to their death, knowing that even in death their tormented bodies would not be granted the sanctuary of a grave. Standing there alone, on the top step of this, their last brief voyage on earth, I felt it my duty to pause and think of them for a moment with heartfelt compassion, in the name of their relatives and friends who, perhaps happy and well, were still alive somewhere in the world.

I left the godforsaken spot and returned to my room. Opening the door, I noticed that the room was not lighted as usual by a strong bulb, but by the flickering light of a single candle. My first impression was that there must be something wrong with the electricity. But then I saw that my associate, the ex-professor of the Szombathely Medical School, was sitting with his elbows on the table, his head resting in his hands, his empty eyes staring at the candle flame, his thoughts a thousand miles away. He did not even notice my presence. The eery light flickered strangely on his face. I touched him lightly on the shoulder:

"Denis," I said softly, "in whose memory did you light a candle here?"

His reply was confused. He mumbled something about his father-in-law and his mother-in-law, both of whom had been dead for fifteen years, and did not even mention his wife and son who, according to the testimony of some of the Sonderkommando members, had perished here. It was easy to see that he was displaying all the symptoms of depressive melancholy and regressive amnesia.

Taking him by the shoulders, I helped him across the room and put him to bed, then stood there, gazing down at him.

Poor friend and learned physician, my sensitive and gentle companion, instead of treating and curing the sick you yourself have fallen beneath the yoke of death, and now belong to death's kingdom. For many months you have witnessed such suffering and horror as the human mind can scarcely conceive, as he who sees cannot believe. Perhaps it is for the best that your nerves have betrayed you, that a benevolent veil of forgetfulness has fallen upon your mind. Now, at least, you need not fret or worry about what the future may hold in store for you.

31 AFTER SEVERAL DAYS OF SILENCE, THE CUS-tomary noises of the crematorium began again. The motors of the big ventilators purred once again, reawakening the furnace flames. The arrival of the Theresienstadt ghetto had been announced.

Since the founding of the Czechoslovakian Republic, Theresienstadt had been primarily a garrison town. The Germans, however, changed the appearance of the city completely, to the point of moving the civilian population away and setting up a model ghetto there. This ghetto housed Jews deported from Austria, Holland and Czechoslovakia itself, about 60,000 in all. The living conditions of the inhabitants were relatively good. They could exercise their professions freely, receive and send mail, and they were aided by the Red Cross. In fact, teams from the International Red Cross paid periodic visits to the little city and, on each occasion, made favorable reports concerning the living conditions and treatment of prisoners.

Thus the Germans got what they wanted from the creation of this model ghetto, for these reports by the International Red Cross had the effect of neutralizing, or better yet, of qualifying as evil slander the rumors going round concerning the horrors of the KZ and the crematoriums.

But now, on the eve of its collapse, the Third Reich ceased to worry any longer about world opinion, and rejected even the mask of its shady humanism. It began to liquidate without delay the Jews still in its custody.

So it was that the turn of the model ghetto at Theresienstadt arrived. When they reached Auschwitz, the still healthy men of this ghetto had the following convocation in their possession:

GOVERNMENTAL SS COMMITTEE OF THE
REICH FOR THE RECRUITING
AND EMPLOYMENT OF SLAVE LABORERS

Notice: The Jew X Y of the Reich protectorate is hereby advised that by order of the abovementioned authority, he has been designated for the Service of Obligatory Labor. The draftee shall, before his departure, deposit his instruments, the tools necessary to the exercise of his profession, a supply of winter clothing, and food enough for one week, with the authority's representative. The date of departure will be announced by public notice.

THERESIENSTADT, THE DATE
Signature

The whole story of obligatory labor was of course an infamous lie, merely a pretext to carry out the liquidation without interruption and to recoup some sorely needed instruments, scarce tools and winter clothing needed by the German populace. Twenty thousand men, fully capable of working and in the full flush of their youth, died in the gas chambers and were incinerated in the crematory ovens. It took 48 hours to exterminate them all. For several days afterwards, silence again reigned in the crematorium.

Two weeks later, still more deportee trains began arriving, in endless succession, at the Jewish ramp. Women and children scrambled out of the box cars. There was no selection. All were directed to the left.

On the floor of the undressing room lay hundreds of tracts, which read:

GOVERNMENTAL SS COMMITTEE OF THE REICH FOR THE RECRUITING AND EMPLOYMENT OF SLAVE LABORERS

Notice: The above-mentioned authority hereby authorizes the wife and children of Jew X Y of the Reich protectorate, called for Obligatory Labor, to join the above-named Jew and to live together with him for the duration of his employment. Suitable lodgings are anticipated. Winter clothing, bedding, and provisions for a week will be furnished by the travelers.

THERESIENSTADT, THE DATE
Signature

As a result of this diabolically conceived notice, twenty thousand women and children who wanted only to ease their husbands' lot, to join their fathers, followed them into the gas chambers and crematory ovens.

32 EARLY IN THE MORNING OF NOVEMBER 17th, 1944, an SS noncommissioned officer came into my room and informed me confidentially that, upon order of higher authority, it was henceforth forbidden to kill any more prisoners, by any means whatsoever, in the KZ. After having witnessed so many lies, I found it impossible to take him at his word, and expressed my doubts on the matter. But he reasserted forcefully that such were the instructions that had been received by radio only a short while before, both at the crematoriums and at the SS political kommando. We would soon see whether or not they were true. Personally, I feared it was only another trick.

Before the end of the morning, however, I had oc-

casion to verify the truth of his statement. A train of
five box cars bearing 500 sick and debilitated prisoners
who thought they were being transferred to a rest camp
stopped on the rails running between number one and
two crematoriums. They were met by an SS political
commission, who conversed at some length with the
commandant and the SS guards accompanying the convoy. At last, before the gates of death, the train was
turned round, and its occupants sent to the F camp hospital barracks.

This was the first time during my stay in the crematoriums that a convoy sent to Auschwitz's "rest camp"
had not been liquidated, either by gas or the *Ober*'s revolver, within an hour after its arrival, but had, on the
contrary, been given medical attention and allowed to
rest in the beds of the camp's hospital barracks.

Scarcely an hour later another train arrived, bearing
500 Slovakian Jews: a group of old people, women,
and young children. They got out of the cars. I watched
carefully for what would follow. Lineup and selection
were the standard order of procedure on the Jewish
ramp. But what I now witnessed was completely out of
keeping with practice. The weary travelers took their
heavy luggage with them when they got down and without exception moved off to the right in the direction
of D Camp. Mothers pushed baby carriages before them,
and the young helped the aged walk. My immediate
reaction was one of enthusiasm. There could be no doubt
about it: the crematorium gates had remained closed before the convoys sent to their death.

For the KZ prisoners the event was a good omen,
giving rise to hope. For the Sonderkommando, however,
the omen was bad, signifying that the end was near. I
was quite sure that the liquidation would be carried out
even before the end of the four-month period.

A new life began in the KZ. There were no more
violent deaths, but the bloody past had to be hidden. The
crematoriums had to be demolished, the pyre ditches
filled in, and any witness to or participant in the horrors
perpetrated here had to disappear. Fully conscious of our
impending doom, we greeted the change with a mixture
of joy and resignation.

Of the millions of souls sent here from the four corners of Europe, by order of the demented Führer, the

pyromaniac of the Third Reich, to be assembled less than an hour before their death on unloading ramps ominously lighted by the butchers of Maydanek, Treblinka, Auschwitz, Birkenau, a few thousand would come out alive.

Feeling uneasy, I paid a return visit about noon to the SS radioman who had informed me of the good news earlier in the day. I wanted to know what decisions had been made in the course of the morning. Had any decision been made concerning the Sonderkommando, and if so, what? Luckily he was alone in the room and I could talk to him freely.

"The Sonderkommando? Why yes," he said affably. "In a few days you'll all be sent to work in an underground war plant not far from Breslau."

I did not believe a word of what he said. For once, however, I knew that his lies were not intended to lull me into a false sense of security. He merely wanted to spare me the bad news, for not so long ago I had cared for him and cured him of a serious illness.

33 IT WAS 2 P.M. I HAD JUST FINISHED LUNCH and was seated by the window of my room, staring at the sky and clouds, that bore the promise of an early snow, when a strident yell from the oven-room passageway broke the silence:

"Alle antreten, alle antreten!"

This was an order we were accustomed to hearing twice a day, in the morning and evening, for muster. Coming at this hour, however, it augured no good.

"Antreten, alle antreten!" the order rang out again, this time more peremptory and impatient than before.

Heavy footsteps resounded just in front of our door. An SS opened it a crack and shouted again: *"Antreten, antreten!"* With sinking hearts we headed for the crematorium courtyard, where a group of well-armed SS already encircled a group of kommando men as we walked up to join them. There was neither surprise nor the faintest sign of protest from anyone. The SS, their machine guns leveled, waited patiently till the last stragglers had joined the group. I glanced around for the last time. The motionless pines that formed a little tunnel at the end of the courtyard were blanketed with snow. All was quiet and very peaceful.

In a few minutes, an order: "To the left, to the left!" We left the courtyard, but instead of going along the road, our guards had us walk towards number two crematorium, directly opposite. We crossed the courtyard of number two, knowing that this would be the last walk we would ever take. They led us into the crematorium furnace room, but none of the SS guards remained inside with us. Instead, they spread out in a circle around the building, stationed at intervals near the doors and windows, their guns poised, ready to fire. The doors were shut and the windows covered with heavy iron bars, completely thwarting any possibility of escape. Our comrades from number two were also present, and a few minutes later they unlocked the door and sent in the kommando from number four. Four hundred and sixty men in all, waiting to die. The only thing we did not know for sure was the method that would be used to exterminate us. We were specialists in the matter, having seen all methods in operation. Would it be in the gas chamber? I hardly thought so, not with the Sonderkommando. Machine guns? Not at all convenient in a room like this. Most likely they intended killing two birds with one stone, that is, blow up the building and us along with it. A plan worthy of the SS. Or perhaps they would toss a phosphorous bomb through one of the windows. That would be an equally effective method, one that had already been tried before, on the deportees from the Milo ghetto. What they had done then was load the deportees into box cars that were so dilapidated as to be of no further use, then toss a bomb inside.

The men of the Sonderkommando were sitting on the concrete floor of the furnace room wherever they could find room, waiting anxiously but silently for the next move.

Suddenly the silence was broken. One of the kommando crew, a thin, sickly, black-haired man about thirty years old whose eyes were magnified by a pair of thick glasses, jumped to his feet and began to speak in a voice loud enough for everyone to hear. It was the "Dayen," the rabbi of a small church community in Poland. A self-taught man, whose knowledge was vast both in the spiritual and temporal realms, he was the ascetic member of the Sonderkommando. In conformance with the tenets of his religion, he ate sparingly, accepting only bread, margarine and onions from the well-stocked kommando larder. He had been assigned to the cremation kommando, but because of his religious fanaticism I had talked the *Ober* into excusing him from this frightful work. The argument I had used with the *Ober* had simply been that this man could not be of much use for the heavy work involved in cremation, since he was weak from his self-imposed, ascetic diet. "Besides," I had argued, "he only slows up the work by pausing over each body to murmur prayers for its salvation. And there are often several thousand souls a day to pray for."

These had been my arguments, but they had sufficed, strangely enough, and the *Ober* had assigned him to burn the pile of refuse which was forever accumulating in the courtyard of number two. This refuse, called "Canada" by the SS, was composed of objects that had once belonged to the deportees, objects of such little material value that they were considered not worth being salvaged: various foodstuffs, documents, diplomas, military decorations, passports, marriage certificates, prayer books, holy objects and Bibles that the deportees had brought with them into captivity.

This little hill called Canada daily consumed hundreds of thousands of photographs—pictures of young married couples, elderly groups, charming children and pretty girls —together with innumerable prayer books, in many of which I found carefully inked notations recording the dates of important events—births, marriages, deaths—in the lives of the various families. Sometimes there were flowers, culled from the graves of beloved parents in all the Jewish cemeteries of Europe, pressed between the pages and piously preserved. Prayer beads and odds and ends of all sorts rounded out the smoldering hill.

This was where the "Dayen" worked, or rather, where he did not work, for all he did was watch the fires burn. Even so he was dissatisfied, for his religious beliefs forbade him from participating in the burning of prayer books or holy objects. I felt sorry for him, but could do nothing

further to help him. It was impossible to obtain an easier
job, for we were, after all, only members of the kommando
of the living dead.

This then was the man who began to speak:

"Fellow Jews. . . . An inscrutable Will has sent our
people to its death; fate has allotted us the cruelest of
tasks, that of participating in our own destruction, of
witnessing our own disappearance, down to the very ashes
to which we are reduced. In no instance have the heavens
opened to send showers and put out the funeral pyre flames.

"We must accept, resignedly, as Sons of Israel should,
that this is the way things must be. God has so ordained
it. Why? It is not for us, miserable humans, to seek the
answer.

"This is the fate that has befallen us. Do not be afraid
of death. What is life worth, even if, by some strange
miracle, we should manage to remain alive? We would
return to our cities and towns to find cold and pillaged
homes. In every room, in every corner, the memory of
those who have disappeared would lurk, haunting our
tear-filled eyes. Stripped of family and relatives, we would
wander like the restless, shuffling shadows of our former
selves, of our completed pasts, finding nowhere any peace
or rest."

Flames burned in his eyes; his thin face was trans-
figured. Perhaps, as he spoke, he was already in touch
with the beyond. Dead silence filled the room, interrupted
only by the occasional scratching of a match as someone
lighted a cigarette. Now and then a heavy sigh expressed
a last farewell bid by one of us to the living and to the
dead.

The heavy doors swung open. Oberschaarführer Steinberg entered the room, accompanied by two guards,
machine guns in hand.

"*Ärzte heraus.* All doctors outside!" he shouted impatiently.

My two colleagues and I, and the lab assistant, left
the room. Steinberg and the two SS soldiers halted half-
way between the two crematoriums. The *Ober* gave me
a sheaf of papers he had been holding in his hand on
which there was a list of numbers and told me to find mine
and strike it out. The papers contained the tattoo numbers
of every man in the Sonderkommando. I took out my pen
and, after hunting for a while, found my number and

drew a line through it. He then told me to do the same
for my comrades. This done, he accompanied us to number
one gate and told us to return to our room, and not to
leave it. We did as ordered.

The following morning a five-truck convoy arrived in
the crematorium courtyard and dumped out its cargo of
bodies, those of the old Sonderkommando. A new group
of thirty men carried them to the incineration room, where
they were laid out in front of the ovens. Terrible burn
scars covered their bodies. Their faces and clothing were
so charred that it was all but impossible to identify them,
especially since their tattoo numbers had disappeared.

After death by gas, on the pyre, by chloroform injections, by a bullet in the back of the neck, by phosphorous bomb, here was a sixth way of killing which I
had not previously discovered.

During the night our comrades had been taken into
a nearby forest and killed by flame throwers. That we
four were still alive did not by any means signify that
they wanted to spare us, but simply that we were still indispensable to them. In allowing us to remain alive, Dr.
Mengele had merely granted us another reprieve. Once
again, the thought gave us neither comfort nor joy.

34 THE SONDERKOMMANDO—THIRTEENTH IN
the history of the crematoriums—had thus
been annihilated. Now our days slipped by
in utter silence and boredom. At loose ends, we wandered
among the cold, forbidding walls. The ringing of my
footsteps in the silence was painful to my ears. We were
given no orders, had nothing to do. At night we lay in
bed, unable to sleep. Only four of us were left in the
building. The thirty men who worked in the crematorium
were not members of the Sonderkommando, but were
quartered in the KZ itself and came here every day only
to burn the bodies of those who had died in the hospital.

Silent, introspective, prostrate with grief, we awaited
our end. It was a bad sign that Oberschaarführer Muss-

feld, as if he had become a different person, studiously
avoided meeting us. Perhaps he felt that he had finished
playing his role: the bloody tragedy was over, and soon
it would be time for the fate that governs the bearers of
forbidden secrets to strike him as well. For days at a time
he remained locked in his room, drinking, with an apparently unquenchable thirst, to forget both the past and
the darkly looming future.

One day Dr. Mengele arrived unexpectedly and came
looking for us in our room, since he guessed that we
would not be in the dissecting room, now that business
was slow. He announced that orders from above had
been received that the Auschwitz KZ would be completely destroyed. No, in the present instance he was not
referring to its inhabitants, but to the institution itself.
Two of the crematoriums would be demolished, the
third would serve temporarily for the cremation of the
hospital's dead. The dissecting room, and we along with
it, would be transferred to number four, which would
continue in operation. Numbers one and two would be
destroyed at once. Number three, of course, had been
completely demolished during the October revolt.

It was both an historic and happy moment when, the
following morning, a kommando of prisoners arrived in
the courtyard and, split up into two groups, began the
demolition of the buildings. Seeing the red brick walls
tumble one after the other under the effect of the dynamite blasts, I had a presentiment of the Third Reich's
own destruction. Jews had built it. Jews were tearing it
down. Never had any KZ prisoners worked with an in-
tensity such as I saw on the faces of those men, whose
expressions reflected the hope of a better life to come.

In the dissecting room, everything movable was packed.
As for the dissection table, only the marble slabs were
dismantled, and replaced by concrete supports. The moving
was finished in a few hours and we spent the night in
number four. After arranging the equipment and setting
up the table—placing the pedestals and cups in position—
the dissecting room was once again ready to function.

For ten days nothing happened. Our indolent life continued. More and more often our SS guards sought refuge
in drunkenness. It was rare that they had their wits about
them for more than a few minutes a day.

One evening while we were eating dinner, Oberschaarführer Mussfeld entered unsteadily, leaned drunkenly on the table and said: *"Guten Abend Jungs . . . Ihr werdet bald alle krepieren, nachher aber kommen wir."* (Good evening, children, soon you're going to die, but afterwards our turn will come.) By these words, spilled from the lips of a drunken man, I learned a truth I had already suspected. Our guards were going to disappear with us.

I offered a glass of tea with a shot of hot rum in it to the *Ober,* who emptied the glasses as fast as we could fill them, with obvious satisfaction. He sat down at our table and, as though he wanted to make up for his past silence, began to talk. He told how his wife had been killed during an air raid, and that his son was on the Russian front.

"It's all over," he said. "The Russians are barely 40 kilometers from Auschwitz. The whole of Germany is in exodus on the highways. Everybody is leaving the frontier areas to seek refuge in the West."

His words did our hearts good. And seeing the *Ober's* despair, a ray of hope began to grow inside me. Perhaps we would after all succeed in leaving here alive.

35 Condemned to that region midway between hope and despair, we safely reached the first of January, 1945. Snow still blanketed the countryside as far as the eye could see. I left the crematorium to take a short walk around the courtyard.

Suddenly the purr of a powerful motor reached my ears, and a moment later a large brown van appeared. Used to transport prisoners, this van was called "Brown Toni" by the camp inmates, for it was painted a dark brownish color. A tall officer got out. I recognized him as Dr. Klein, an SS major, one of the evil, bloody-handed KZ officials. I came to attention and gave him the regulation salute. He had brought a hundred new victims from KZ Barracks number 10, that is, the camp prison.

"Here's some work to start the New Year with," he

told the *Ober* who hurried up to greet him.

The Ober was so drunk he could hardly stand up. He had apparently gone all out celebrating the New Year. Who knows, perhaps he had merely been steeling himself against the guards' impending end. At any rate, it was evident from his expression that he was not at all pleased to learn he had been given a bloody job to perform on New Year's Day. A hundred Polish prisoners, Christian men all, had been brought here to be murdered. SS guards took them to an empty room next to the furnace room and ordered them to undress immediately. Dr. Klein and the *Ober,* meanwhile, took a stroll around the courtyard.

I hastened to where the prisoners were undressing and began questioning them as to the reasons for their imprisonment. One of them told me he had given refuge to one of his relatives, at his home in Krakau. The Gestapo had accused him of aiding partisans and brought him to trial before a court-martial. While awaiting sentence, he had been sent to Barracks 10. Although he did not yet know it, the court had already condemned him to death. That was why he was here. He was under the mistaken impression, however, that he had been brought here for a shower before being assigned to a forced labor battalion.

Another had been imprisoned for having aided and abetted inflation. A serious offense, to be sure. Just what had his crime been? Why, he had bought a pound of butter on the black market. A third had been jailed for having wandered into a forbidden zone. They had accused him of being a partisan spy. It was much the same story everywhere I asked: minor slips and infractions of the law turned into fabulous, trumped-up charges.

Now that there was no longer any Sonderkommando, the SS guards led the men to the *Ober*'s revolver.

Again, the sound of "Brown Toni's" powerful motor. A hundred new victims arrived, all women, quite well dressed. They were sent to the same room where, only a few minutes before, the men had undressed. Then one by one the women were also taken to the *Ober*'s waiting gun. They too were Polish Christians; they too paid with their lives for minor infractions of the law.

The cremation was carried out by the SS, who asked me to furnish them with rubber gloves for the job.

As soon as he had made quite certain, *in viso,* that

the 200 prisoners had been duly executed, Dr. Klein left the crematorium. There was nothing contradictory about the order of November 17th forbidding the practice of violent death, and today's slaughter. On the contrary, all the SS had just done was to carry out the sentences tendered by a duly constituted court-martial.

36 MY DAYS PASSED QUIETLY, WITHOUT INTERRUPTION. It was rumored that Dr. Mengele had fled Auschwitz. The KZ had a new doctor, and, what was more, from now on the area was no longer to be called KZ, but "Arbeitslager," that is, "Work Camp." Everything was breaking up and falling to pieces.

On the first of January a newspaper I happened to come across told of the beginning of the Russian offensive. The noise of heavy artillery rattled the windowpanes; the line of fire grew closer every day. On January 17th I went to bed early, although I was not tired. I wanted to be alone with my thoughts. Lulled by the agreeable warmth of a coke stove, I soon drifted off.

It must have been about midnight. I was awakened by a series of powerful blasts, the crackling of machine-gun fire, and dazzling flashes. I heard the sound of doors banging and footsteps running. I jumped out of bed and opened the door. The furnace room lights were on, and the doors of the SS' rooms were wide open, witness to the speed of their departure.

The crematorium's heavy gate were also open. Not a guard in sight. I glanced quickly at the watch towers. For the first time in months they were empty. I ran back to wake up my companions. We dressed in haste and got ready for the great journey. The SS had fled. We would not stay here a minute longer, here where for eight months Death had lain in wait for us every minute of every hour. We could not wait for the Russians, since we risked falling into the hands of the SS rear guard, who would not hesitate

to execute us. Luckily we had excellent clothing—sweaters
overcoats, shoes—which meant a great deal, for the temperature was at least 10 below zero. We each took a
two-pound can of food, and filled our pockets with medicines and cigarettes. We left, filled with the feverish sensa-
tion of liberation. Direction: The Birkenau KZ, two
kilometers from the crematoriums. Immense flames glowed
along the horizon there. It was probably the KZ burning

Crossing the furnace room, we passed in front of the
room where the gold was stored. Boxes containing untold wealth still lay inside, but we did not even think of
stopping to take some of it. What was money when one's
life was at stake? We had learned that nothing lasts and
that no value is absolute. The only exception to that rule
freedom.

We left by the main gate. No one stopped us. The
abrupt change seemed incredible. Our path led through
the little forest of Birkenau, whose trees were covered
from trunk to top with a heavy layer of glistening snow
The same path down which millions had walked on their
way to death. . . . We passed beside the Jewish ramp
buried in the snow. And here they had climbed down
from the boxcars for selection. . . . The image of the
two columns, left and right, separated forever, gazing
sadly across at those they had just left, came back to
me. But for all of them, the matter had merely been one
of chronological order: they were all dead.

Yes, the Birkenau KZ was on fire. Some of the guards'
rooms, in which the camp records were stored, were burning. A large crowd, perhaps, 3,000, was gathered in front
of the camp gate waiting for the order to leave. Without
hesitation I joined their ranks. No one knew me here. I
was no longer the bearer of unholy secrets, no longer a
member of the Sonderkommando, and therefore did not
have to die. Here I was merely another KZ prisoner, lost
in the crowd. It seemed to me this was the best solution.
My colleagues concurred. Everyone was fleeing Birkenau,
but I judged it improbable that they would be able to take
us very far. In a day or two the Russians would catch up
with us. But sometime before that happened, the SS would
desert. Meanwhile, our best bet was to march with the
others between the two lines of fire.

It was about one o'clock in the morning. The last SS
had left the camp. He closed the iron gates and cut off

the lights from the main switchboard, which was located near the entrance. The enormous cemetery of European Judaism, Birkenau, sank into darkness. My eyes lingered for a long while on the barbed wires of the camp and the rows of barracks that stood out against the night. Farewell, cemetery of millions, cemetery without a single grave!

We set out, surrounded by a company of SS. We discussed with our new-found friends all that had happened, and what might happen now, trying to guess what the morrow would bring. Would the SS succeed in escorting our convoy to a new prison, or would they, as we hoped, desert us somewhere along the way?

We had walked for approximately five kilometers when our left flank became the target of a deadly fire. The Russian advance guard had seen us and, mistaking us for a military column, opened fire. They were using submachine guns and had the support of a light tank. The SS returned the fire and shouted for us to take cover on the ground. We crawled into the ditches on either side of the road. The fire was heavy on both sides. Then, in a little while, all grew quiet again and we resumed our journey across the sterile, snow-covered earth of Silesia.

Slowly it began to grow light. I estimated that we had covered about 15 kilometers during the night. But still we marched across the packed snow. All along the way I noticed pots and blankets and wooden shoes that had been abandoned by a convoy of women who had preceded us.

A few kilometers farther on we came upon a much sadder sight: every forty or fifty yards, a bloody body lay in the ditch beside the road. For kilometers and kilometers it was the same story: bodies everywhere. Exhausted, they had been unable to walk any farther; when they had strayed from the ranks, an SS had dispatched them with a bullet in the back of the head.

So I had not left murder and violence behind me. Apparently the SS had been ordered not to leave any victims behind. A discouraging thought. The sight of the bodies made a deep impression on all of us, and we quickened our pace. To walk meant to live.

Now the first shots began sounding in our own convoy as well. The bodies of two fellow-sufferers fell into the ditches. Unable to advance another step, they had sat down: a bullet in the neck. Ten minutes did not go by without the same thing recurring.

Towards noon we reached Plesow, where we made our first stop. We spent an hour in a sports stadium. Anyone who had some food ate a little. We smoked a cigarette, then set off again along the snowy road, feeling greatly refreshed. But a week went by, two, and still we walked. For twenty days we walked, till at last we reached a railway station. In all, we had covered over 200 kilometers, having had almost nothing to eat for three weeks. At night we slept outdoors, in the bitter cold. When we arrived at Ratibor only 2,000 of us were left. About a thousand had been shot along the way. We were all relieved to see the line of box cars waiting for us.

We climbed into the cars and, after an all-night wait, began to move. The trip lasted five days. I did not count the number of comrades who froze to death, but only 1,500 of us reached our destination, the Mauthausen KZ. Some of the missing 500 were not dead, however, for there were a few who, taking advantage of a propitious occasion, fled the convoy and perhaps escaped.

37 THE MAUTHAUSEN KZ SAT ON TOP OF A hill overlooking the ancient city of the same name. This extermination camp, which resembled a fortified town, was made of granite blocks. With its bastions, its towers and loopholes, it looked from afar like a medieval castle.

This picture would have been a rare and beautiful one if only the stones had been covered with a century-old growth of lichen, or streaked gray from the constant play of wind and rain and snow through the years. Instead, they presented a façade of dazzling white that clashed with the surrounding landscape, which was crowned with dark forests. For the "castle" had only recently been built and its walls were not yet marked with that austere beauty of ancient buildings. The Third Reich had had it constructed as a KZ. Forty thousand Spanish Republicans, refugees in France, had been brought here after the occupation, as well as hundreds of thousands of German Jews. It was they who had worked in the Mauthausen quarries cutting the blocks; it was they who had carried the finished stones along the seven-kilometer path up the mountain, where formerly only wild goats had grazed. And it was they who had constructed the powerful walls around their house of sorrow, which was composed of wooden barracks. They had finished the castle at the price of unbelievable suffering, but they had never lived to occupy it. In the midst of this great mass of stone and concrete they had all perished, like the slaves in ancient Egypt.

The camp had not remained unoccupied for very long, however. Thousands who had fought in the Yugoslav underground, as well as members of all the various resistance movements throughout Europe—plus, of course, Europe's doomed race, the Jews—had flocked here by the tens of thousands, filling the fortress' barracks in a matter of days. There they had lived during the brief period preceding their death.

Now another convoy, ours, decimated by the long trip and the insufferable cold, slowly wended its way up the arduous, snow-covered mountain path. Our strength all but gone, we at last entered the gates of the KZ and lined up, in the gathering dusk, on the "Appelplatz."

I looked around for my companions. Fischer, the lab assistant, was missing. I had not seen him since Plesow. Then he had been lying in the snow, his strength completely spent. From his contracted facial expression, I had suspected that his end was near. He was fifty-five and had spent five years in the KZ, so it was not surprising that his organism had been unequal to the long walk and paralyzing cold. Dr. Korner was in pretty good shape, but Dr. Gorog, on the other hand, was in a critical condition. His mental troubles had steadily worsened, and even in the days of the crematorium keeping his condition a secret had been a source of constant worry to me. I had done all I could to make sure he never ran into Dr. Mengele. Mussfeld had also been dangerous. If either one had noticed his condition, his life would not have been worth a penny. Before leaving the crematorium he had already informed me of his last wishes.

"Nicholas," he had said, "you are a strong-willed person and one day you'll manage to get out of all this alive. As for me, I know I'm finished." I had tried to protest, but he had waved my words of encouragement aside and gone on: "I have proof that my wife and daughter both died in the gas chamber. But I left my twelve-year-old son with the monks of the Koszeg cloister. If you ever do get home, fetch him and bring him up as your own. I say this in full possession of all my faculties, knowing I haven't long to live."

I had promised him that I would faithfully carry out his wishes, in the event I escaped and he did not.

Now, happily, we had left the site of certain death far behind. To die now, so near to the end of the road, just when the hope of freedom had filled our hearts, would be truly tragic.

Following roll call, we were sent through a tortuous passage to the baths. There we joined groups newly arrived from other camps: there must have been 10,000 of us crammed into this small area. A strong wind whistled between the walls of the castle. The mountain on which the camp was perched marked the beginning of the Alps, and the winters here were extremely rigorous. We learned that we would be taken into the baths in groups of forty. At that rate, I calculated it would take three days for everybody to bathe.

The guards stationed here had been recruited from among German criminals, men serving terms for murder, larceny and the like. Needless to say, they were the faithful servants of the SS. Today their job consisted of grouping the deportees for the baths. Aryan prisoners went first. In fact there were so many Aryans that I figured the Jews' turn would not come before the third day. To wait here for two days became a matter of life and death, for a prisoner could not enter the barracks and get himself enrolled on the list of those to be fed without first passing through the baths. For a person who was already exhausted, a two-day wait without food would mean almost certain death, for either his legs would buckle or his eyelids would yield to sleep, and he would sink into the hard-packed snow, never again to rise. Already about a hundred prisoners were lying on the ground around me. No one was paying any attention to them, for each had all he could do to save himself. This was our final sprint towards the finish line of Life.

Reflecting on my situation, I decided that I could not spend the night outdoors without seriously imperiling my chances for survival. I had to get into the baths today.

Poor Denis was wandering aimlessly about, hatless, without his glasses, like a man asleep. His gaze was troubled and he was muttering unintelligible words to himself as he walked. I took him by the arm and dragged him with me, hoping that I could somehow get us both into the baths. But before we had gone more than a few steps he slipped away and was lost in the seething mass of humanity. I called his name, shouting at the top of my lungs, but to no avail. The wind was so strong I could hardly hear my own voice.

Sensing the danger, I forced my way through the crowd and approached the steps leading down into the baths. At last I worked my way to the front row. Several SS armed with rubber clubs were guarding the entrance. A group of forty people was already assembled, waiting to go in. They were all Aryans.

Once again I made a snap decision: leaving the crowd I approached an SS Oberscharführer and addressed him in a self-assured tone of voice:

"Herr Oberscharführer, I'm the doctor for the Auschwitz convoy. Let me into the baths."

He looked me over. My respectable clothes, perhaps my determined manner, or, more likely, my perfect command of German seemed to make an impression on him. At any rate, turning to his colleagues posted near the entrance, he said: "Let the doctor go inside."

I descended alone, preceding the group of forty who were waiting beside the stairway. Safe! And how easy it had been! Yes, sometimes it pays to make up one's mind on the spur of the moment.

The warm air of the baths soon lent new strength to my almost frozen legs. After days and days of cold, at long last a warm room! The bath itself also did me a world of good. Our clothes were considered contaminated, and we had to give them up. I was sorry to hand over my overcoat, my suit and my warm woolen sweater, but at least was happy to see that they let me keep my shoes. A good pair of shoes could easily be an important factor in saving one's life in the KZ.

I put my shoes back on and rejoined the group that had just finished bathing. Otherwise naked, we started back towards the path leading to the baths, where we waited for half an hour till there were enough of us to fill an entire barracks. After a warm bath, to remain outside in an icy wind, with the temperature close to zero, was to flirt with death.

At length another group of forty joined us and we started off. The SS guard made us keep in step as we walked, but after marching only 50 yards we reached Barracks 33 of the quarantine camp.

A prisoner, wearing the familiar green insignia of a criminal offender, was posted in front of the entrance: our barracks chief. He handed every newcomer a fourth of a loaf of bread; a little farther on a clerk slapped a spoonful of margarine, made of meat fat, on the bread. We were also given half a pint of steaming hot coffee.

After 10 days of privation this seemed like a royal feast. Having downed my food, I looked around for a likely place to lie down, and finally settled on a secluded corner, where I judged that my chances of being walked on would be fairly slim. I lay on the floor, for there were no beds in the quarantine camp. Nevertheless, I slept soundly until reveille.

Waking, my first thoughts were for those still standing— provided they were still able to stand—in the freezing cold, waiting to get into the baths.

We stayed in Barracks 33 for three days, during which we had nothing to do. Our food was not too bad and we were thus more or less able to recuperate from our three-week march.

On the third day of our stay an SS officer, accompanied by a general, visited our barracks and ordered anyone who had formerly worked in the Auschwitz KZ to step forward.

My blood froze in my veins. Methodical race that they are, the Germans no doubt had a muster list containing the names or numbers of those who had worked at Auschwitz. It seemed likely. And yet . . . thinking about it, I came to the conclusion that this was merely a ruse, an attempt to single out from the mass those capable of revealing the sordid mysteries of the crematoriums. If they had really had a list all they would have had to do was to check our tattoo numbers. No one knew me here. I waited, the blood pounding in my ears; there was complete silence in the barracks as the seconds ticked slowly by. And then they left. I had won again. Once again the wheel of death had spun and passed me by.

That night we were given the striped jerkin of pris-ners and taken by the mountain path to the Mauthausen railway station. There we were loaded into the inevitable boxcars, 7,000 souls in all, and sent to the Melk an der Donau concentration camp. It was only a short journey and, for a change, fairly comfortable, that is, we were not tacked in like sardines but had room enough to sit on the floor. Three hours after we had climbed into the cars we climbed down again.

The Melk KZ, like that of Mauthausen, sat on the crest of a hill overlooking the surrounding countryside. Originally a prison, bearing the name of Freiherr Von Birabo, its immense barracks were large enough to accommodate 15,000 criminals at a time. The picturesque beauty of the countryside mitigated our pain and discomfort: the enormous, baroque-style monastery projected from the rocky hill, and, below, the Danube wound continuously on its way, forming a picture of unforgettable beauty. The Danube was a river we associated with our home and country. Seeing it now made us feel that home was not quite so far away.

38 THE SPRING OF 1945 CAME EARLY. IT WAS now the beginning of April, and the trees that rose from the ditches lining the barbed-wire fences of Melk were already green. On the banks of the Danube a green carpet replaced the snow, only patches of which remained to remind us of the severe winter through which we had just passed.

I had been living in the KZ for eight weeks, through good days and bad, but the experience had sapped my strength and left me tired and weak. Only the hope of an early liberation kept me from slipping into a state of utter lethargy and indifference.

Here everything was disintegrating. The final phases of the Third Reich's collapse were unfolding before our eyes. Defeated armies passed in interminable columns towards the interior of a country already reduced to smoking ruins. On the Danube, whose waters were swollen from the melting snows, hundreds of boats and barges transported the inhabitants of evacuated cities. The Third Reich's dream of a millennium was crumbling. The conviction of a people born to rule, of a Master Race, was giving way to bitter disillusionment. The peoples of Europe, avid for freedom, no longer lived in the fear that their own town or city might, by a simple, arbitrary stroke of the conqueror's pen, be wiped off the map; there was no longer any danger of seeing their homes plundered, of having themselves stripped of all they owned, of feeling the needlepoint tattoo numbers on their arms, of being shipped to forced labor camps and guarded by police dogs and SS troops whose badge was the death's head.

The pyromaniacs of the Third Reich were now playing their final scene on the stage of the world: they who had set the world aflame were now perishing in their own fires. The raucous-voiced corporal, whose words, "Deutschland Über Alles" had been heard on the wavelengths of the entire world for over a decade, was now trembling in his underground bunker. The uncompromising pride of the Third Reich had been broken by the world-wide collaboration of people not avid of conquest, but of freedom.

On April 7th, 1945, the string of arc lights set on top of the poles to which the barbed wires were fastened did not come on. Darkness and silence closed in on the abandoned spot. The camp was empty, the gate closed. The 7,000 prisoners had been taken farther inland, first by boat, then along the roads swarming with refugees. For seven long days and nights we traveled, till at last we reached our new destination, the Ebensee concentration camp, the fourth KZ through whose yawning gates I had passed.

Upon arrival, the inevitable and interminable roll call. Then the bath. And then again the quarantine camp, with its filthy barracks, its guards armed with rubber clubs, its hard floor. I blindly submitted to these three customary phases. During roll call a cold wind was blowing and a driving rain soaked my clothes. Bitterness overwhelmed me. I knew that it could only be a matter of days before we were liberated, but for the moment we were still living in a world of confusion and indecision. And yet, when the moment for decision finally arrived, perhaps it would be an ill-starred one for us all. The end of our captivity could quite conceivably turn into a bloody tragedy: they might kill us all before the impending moment of liberation arrived. After twelve months of imprisonment, at a time when all law had ceased to exist, such an end would indeed be in keeping with the customs of the Third Reich.

But such was not the case. On May 5th a white flag flew from the Ebensee watch tower. It was finished. They had laid down their arms. The sun was shining brightly when, at nine o'clock, an American light tank, with three soldiers aboard, arrived and took possession of the camp.

We were free.

EPILOGUE

SICK AT HEART, AND PHYSICALLY ILL, I started my long voyage homeward. The trip was not a pleasant one: everywhere I looked I saw, where flourishing cities and towns had once stood, nothing but gutted ruins and the collective, white-crossed graves of the dead.

I dreaded the truth, fearing to return to an empty, plundered home, a home where neither parents nor wife, daughter nor sister, would be waiting to greet me with warmth and affection. Persecution and sorrow, the horrors of the crematorium and funeral pyres, my eight months in the kommando of the living dead, had dulled my sense of good and evil.

I felt that I should rest, try to regain my strength. But, I kept asking myself, for what? On the one hand, illness racked my body; on the other, the bloody past froze my heart. My eyes had followed countless innocent souls to the gas chambers, witnessed the unbelievable spectacle of the funeral pyres. And I myself, carrying out the orders of a demented doctor, had dissected hundreds of bodies, so that a science based on false theories might benefit from the deaths of those millions of victims. I had cut the flesh of healthy young girls and prepared nourishment for the mad doctor's bacteriological cultures. I had immersed the bodies of dwarfs and cripples in calcium chloride, or had them boiled so that the carefully prepared skeletons might safely reach the Third Reich's museums to justify, for future generations, the destruction of an entire race. And even though all this was now past, I would still have to cope with it in my thoughts and dreams. I could never erase these memories from my mind.

At least twice I had felt the wings of death brush by me: once, prostrate on the ground, with a company of SS trained in the art of summary execution poised above me, I had escaped unharmed. But three thousand of my friends, who had also known the terrible secrets of the crematoriums, had not been so lucky. I had marched for hundreds of kilometers through fields of snow, fighting the cold, hunger, and my own exhaustion, merely to reach another concentration camp. The road I had traveled had indeed been long.

Now, home again, nothing. I wandered aimlessly through silent rooms. Free, but not from my bloody past, nor from the deep-rooted grief that filled my mind and gnawed at my sanity. And the future seemed just as dark. I walked like my own ghost, a restless figure in the once familiar streets. The only times I managed to shake off my state of depression and lethargy was when, mistakenly, I thought for a fleeting second that someone I saw or briefly encountered on the street was a member of my family.

One afternoon, several weeks after my return, I felt chilly and sat down near the fireplace, hoping to derive a little comfort from the cheerful glow that filled the room. It grew late; dusk was falling. The doorbell roused me from my daydreams. Before I could get up to answer it my wife and daughter burst into the room!

They were in good health and had just been freed from Bergen-Belsen, one of the most notorious of the extermination camps. But that was as much as they were able to tell me before breaking down. For hours they sobbed uncontrollably. I was content just to hold them in my arms, while the flood of their grief flowed from their tortured minds and hearts. Their sobs, a language I was well familiar with, slowly subsided.

We had much to do, much to relate, much to rebuild. I knew it would take much time and infinite patience before we could resume any sort of really normal life. But all that mattered was that we were alive . . . and together again. Life suddenly became meaningful again. I would begin practicing, yes . . . But I swore that as long as I lived I would never lift a scalpel again. . . .